BRIAN MA...   ...ve
critical studie...   ...d
to write the f...   ...s
in Britain. His ...   ...u.r. Benson, from Marie
from John As...   ...ranged
Corelli to Georgiana Duchess of Devonshire. He has
also rescued twentieth-century society hostesses from
footnotes into a book of their own, and traced the
origins of the ruling family of Udaipur in India. His
penetrating study of mass murderer Dennis Nilsen,
Killing for Company, won the Gold Dagger Award
for non-fiction in 1985, after which he found himself
invited to lecture on murderers as well as dukes,
gorillas and hostesses. He is also the author of
the highly-acclaimed *The Shrine of Jeffrey Dahmer*.
Masters is well-known for his interviews in the *Sunday
Telegraph*, and he reviews regularly for that paper as
well as *The Spectator* and the *Mail on Sunday*.

Also by Brian Masters

Molière
Sartre
Saint-Exupéry
Rabelais
Camus – A Study
Wynyard Hall and the Londonderry Family
Dreams about H.M. The Queen
The Dukes
Now Barabbas Was A Rotter: The Extraordinary Life of
Marie Corelli
The Mistresses of Charles II
Georgiana, Duchess of Devonshire
Great Hostesses
Killing for Company: The Case of Dennis Nilsen
The Swinging Sixties
The Passion of John Aspinall
Maharana – the Udaipur Dynasty
Gary
The Life of E.F. Benson
Voltaire's Treatise on Tolerance
(Edited and translated)
The Shrine of Jeffrey Dahmer

On Murder

Brian Masters

CORONET BOOKS
Hodder and Stoughton

First published in 1994 by Hodder and Stoughton
A division of Hodder Headline PLC
A Coronet paperback

10 9 8 7 6 5 4 3 2 1

British Library Cataloguing in Publication Data

Masters, Brian
On Murder
I. Title
364.1523

ISBN 0 340 59826 3

Typeset by Phoenix Typesetting, Ilkley, West Yorkshire.

Printed and bound in Great Britain by
Cox & Wyman Ltd, Reading

Hodder and Stoughton Ltd
A Division of Hodder Headline PLC
338 Euston Road
London NW1 3BH

For my brother, Colin Masters

CONTENTS

INTRODUCTION

It is a commonplace to hear that murder is "fascinating", whether it be in the pub, the club, or the drawing-room. Addictive or repetitive murder (sometimes safely called "serial" murder, hiding its true nature behind an adjective of bland and harmless intent) is especially enticing, because it permits a *frisson* of excitement in the contemplation of unimaginable wickedness, coupled with the secure knowledge that such wickedness cannot, need not, and indeed should not, be understood. By careful operation of this kind of doublethink, it is possible actually to *enjoy* the narrative of murder in an entirely guiltless vacuum, poring over the details of hideous crimes, at the same time protected from the necessity of trying to work out why they occurred by seeing the world through the murderer's eyes. This is not so much hypocrisy as mental and moral laziness.

I distrust the word "fascination" in this context. It suggests an unwary and unreflective hypnotic trance, the refuge of the voyeur. There is a vicariousness about the posture of being fascinated by murder which is both unhealthy and untrue; it is much harder, more demanding on the psyche, and more true, to be *interested* in murder. This, however, requires a step inwards and downwards which most people are afraid to take. Easier, therefore, to remain simply fascinated.

Readers have sometimes mistaken my admitted curiosity and inquisitiveness on the subject as evidence of (perhaps dangerous?) obsession. The fact that I will not evade the stark nastiness of a murderous attack, nor, at the same

time, shirk the duty to seek the personality of the attacker, smacks of prurience on the one hand, naivety on
the other. Yet the libraries of medical schools are stacked
high with learned journals which must needs make the
same approach, and their authors do not find their motives
questioned. *Medicine, Science and the Law, The Journal of
Clinical Psychopathy, The American Journal of Psychiatry*,
and many more, contain essays and studies which set out
precisely to examine the gruesome results of compulsive
murder and, thereby, to study the mind of the man who
could do such a thing. They even have photographs of the
victims of attack which would never be allowed in a more
generally available publication. These good doctors are not
"fascinated" – they are mystified, and their work attests to
an urgent need to dispel the mystery.

Not being a professional, I cannot attain their degree
of objectivity and detachment, though the effort must be
made. My lapse in this regard was brought home to me in
a conversation I had with Dennis Nilsen, shortly after his
conviction. I told him that I thought I could understand how
murder might happen, what long-festering causes might
precipitate it, what anguish and despair might follow it, even
what distorted emotions might, for a brief moment, make it
appear a "good" thing rather than a "bad" thing. But I could
not for the life of me understand how he, the murderer,
could subsequently spend a whole weekend cutting up the
body into small two-inch pieces, slicing off thighs, boiling
heads until the flesh stuck to the sides of the saucepan, and
still face himself with equanimity. That, I said, was what
divorced him from the rest of humankind, and made him
unrecognisable – not the murders, but the defilement of
corpses. Nilsen looked at me almost in disbelief. "There's
something very wrong with your morals," he said. "They're
upside down. The unforgivable thing I did was to squeeze
the life out of a living person, to rob him of his future. Once
he was dead, he was only a corpse, a thing, which could

not suffer or be hurt. Nothing I did afterwards could be seen as wrong, merely pragmatic. If you are more offended by what I did to corpses than what I did to living people, then you're really in trouble."

Of course, his remarks gave me pause to wonder. Pathologists hold a similarly dispassionate view of the objects they must dissect, and they are right to do so, in so far as the attitude must go with the job; a pathologist who burst into tears at the sight of a once pretty young girl reduced to ugly pulp in a road accident would not last long. But a chasm separates him from Nilsen. The pathologist is not indifferent to the pity of death; he must conquer his humanity in the service of scientific discipline. The murderer was genuinely perplexed that I should feel horror at the notion of dismemberment, because he lacked that oh-so-deeply rooted reverence towards the dead which is an essential part of our species. Of course one cannot harm a corpse, so why not fling it over the rooftops? Westerners bury their dead, the Hindus burn them on funeral pyres, others leave them ceremoniously to the vultures, but in each case the corpse is given back to the world to renew the cycle of birth and death, to become another element (earth, fire, flesh) in that same world in which it once lived. There is respect in this, both for life and for our place within the endless circle. There is no respect in cutting a body into pieces and flushing it down the lavatory.

Though it may be illogical to be upset by the murderer's treatment of a corpse, it is human, of a humanity ascending to the very first emergence of our species from the drifting herds of our forebears. This important legacy is missing from the addictive murderer, he is too logical, and by his logic he is mad, by which we mean unlike us.

The world's great literature addresses the psychology of the murderer as readily as it does that of the adulterer or the saint. *Macbeth, King Lear, Titus Andronicus* are replete with the contemplation of killing and its crippling of the soul. Aeschylus and Euripides show us the depths to which the gods can make us sink. Racine and Dostoevsky take us right into the heart of people struggling with the poisons of revenge, passion or insanity. None of them is "fascinated" by murder, but they all acknowledge it as part of the human condition. The Marquis de Sade *was* fascinated, which is why his books are so shallow.

While it would be arrogant nonsense to pretend that a book of true crime should be considered in the same paragraph as the great luminaries of literature, there is no reason why it should not at least aspire to the same approach towards its subject, one of attention and thoroughness of mind. The examination of true crime is necessarily limited. One may learn a great deal from the careers of murderers in history, from Lacenaire (whom, incidentally, Dostoevsky studied), to Jack the Ripper, but one cannot, on the whole, get anywhere near the allusive subtlety of the artist who has the freedom to invent and embellish. Ultimately, then, we learn more from Macbeth than we can ever learn from Ted Bundy. But there is no reason why one should not try to stretch the genre beyond its lamentably narrow limits. It is frankly appalling that so few writers of true crime even make the attempt. The books tumble off the shelf, there are so many, but open them and they are empty.

It is a terrible paradox that even the murderer may be aware of this, as is suggested by another story relating to Dennis Nilsen. He had no editorial influence over *Killing for Company*, and had no idea what I had written or how I had treated the material. However, I thought it reasonable to show him a proof copy before publication. When next we met, he said that he had promised not to interfere, but would I mind if he made two comments? I had no objection to hearing what he had to say. "You have gone into all 15 murders," he said, "and you have identified none of them. I know why. You want to protect the relatives from exposure to grisly details they may not wish to know. But you are left with *only* the grisly details if you don't tell us who these people are. If you want your book to reach a better audience than the plastic-mac brigade, you should select only half a dozen murders, or it gets repetitive and salacious, and you should identify the victims. The reader will then be interested, and will think more about it." Oddly enough, it was the same advice I had received from my editor.

All murder is awful. Most are the product of domestic squabbles, as every statistician or policeman will tell you, and only a very few result from a mental derangement which courts and psychiatrists alike are reluctant to recognise, for entirely understandable social reasons. But we may still look at them, and at ourselves, and ponder. "The proper study of mankind is man." Murderers are men, too.

CHAPTER 1

Dennis Nilsen

The trial of Dennis Nilsen took place in Number One court at the Old Bailey in October 1983. It attracted a huge amount of attention because the charges depicted a monster of unfathomable depravity, yet the man himself stubbornly eluded cheap and simple classification. Nilsen faced eight charges in all: six of murder and two of attempted murder. Had the police been able to gather sufficient evidence, he would doubtless have faced more charges, but some of those he had killed, butchered and burnt on bonfires had been obliterated beyond trace, save for a few fragments of bone amongst the topsoil of his back garden, and many of these sad young men would for ever remain unidentified. It was estimated that he had killed 15 times, though this may be an exaggeration. (He had scribbled out a list of what he could remember on a scrap of paper in the police cell.) Certainly, at least 12 men had died at his hands. There had been no case like it in British criminal history.

Nilsen was not called to give evidence. The only words he uttered were "Not guilty" when the indictment was read out to him, although this did not presume a denial of the facts, only a denial of criminal responsibility for them. "We are not dealing with murder here, though I have killed," he wrote. Even this was a late development in his eight months of remand. He had originally intended to plead guilty, and had instructed his solicitor, Ronald Moss, to that effect. There were two reasons for this, one self-regarding, the other consistent with some sense of remorse. In the first place, he did not wish to plead insanity, as he felt he had known precisely what he was doing and at no time could claim to have been acting in obedience to voices or strange hallucinations. Secondly, he knew that a guilty plea would ensure that the trial was over in one day, as there would be no necessity for the police to present detailed and disgusting evidence; he was especially concerned about the two men who would be required to give evidence on the attempted murder charges, Carl Stottor and Paul Nobbs, and would need to re-enact, in a public forum, their hideous experiences. Hence the intention to plead guilty. Within the last three weeks, however, Nilsen had changed his solicitor and would now be represented by Ralph Haeems. It was decided to enter a plea of diminished responsibility.

The public appetite to know more about Nilsen, what sort of man he was, what had been his history, who had been his friends, was frustrated, quite correctly, by the English concept of contempt of court. From his arrest in February until his conviction in November there had been no mention of his case or his character, lest such publicity should interfere with the course of justice. Even in the trial, it seemed, his voice was not to be heard, except at one remove when his confession was read out by Detective Chief Superintendent Chambers to a court rigid with incredulous attention. The only personal moments which enabled press and public to imagine, to some extent at least, what an encounter with this man may have been like, were when Nobbs and Stottor told the court how he had started to kill them, by strangulation or drowning, and stopped. Stottor in particular reduced the Old Bailey to pitiful silence as he recalled how he had been held under water in a bathtub, had pleaded for mercy, then resigned himself to dying.

The jury retired on 3 November and returned their verdict on the following day, having failed initially to agree and been ordered by the judge to resume deliberations.

Mr Justice Croom-Johnson eventually agreed to accept majority verdicts. By ten to two, Nilsen was found guilty on all counts of murder and one count of attempted murder. On the remaining count of attempted murder, the jury was unanimous in its decision: guilty. The plea of diminished responsibility was rejected, and Nilsen was sent to prison for life, with a recommendation he serve no less than 25 years. Dennis Nilsen was led away to well-deserved oblivion.

There was yet, however, one way in which his voice would be heard, filtered through somebody else's interpretations. Twice a week for eight months I had been visiting Nilsen at Brixton Prison, and had seen him after each day's proceedings throughout the trial. He had in addition written me about 150 letters, and had kept a prison journal running to 50 volumes of exercise books, for my exclusive use. I was collecting material for a study of the case, which would be published nearly two years later under the title *Killing for Company*, and I was known therefore to have privileged access to the murderer. Hence, if the press could not talk to him, they would instead listen to me.

It was thus that the first article of the three which follow came to be written. Published just two days after the verdict, it attempted to satisfy some of the public hunger for a glimpse of this extraordinary individual who could retain an impudent and somewhat discomfiting sense of humour even amidst the revelation of his awfulness; it was not pride or cheek, but a parallel strain of character which existed independently of his crimes – a sort of irrepressible jokiness. I wanted also to bring into relief the dim glimmer of remorse that he evinced, and to indicate what his state of mind was as he contemplated a lifetime of incarceration. But the piece is not in any sense profound, nor does it address the moral implications of what I was doing.

These were twofold. The question of moral responsibility which the writer should feel *towards* his subject and in the presence of a murderer is a provocative one, which I shall save to a later chapter. The other question, as to whether exposure to evil can be contaminating, whether as a spokesman for a killer I become his accomplice, and whether the writer's responsibility towards the reader should be protective, was one which increasingly preoccupied me as the book went to press and Nilsen's belongings arrived, on his instructions, in my house.

The second article, "Is Evil Contagious?", deals with these matters up to a point and reflects my growing anxieties, which continued to disconcert me afterwards and have yet to be totally dispelled. The third piece is a conversation with the Earl of Longford some six years later, wherein we again debate evil, its influence, and the possibility of resisting it or being delivered from it. Lord Longford had, of course, been visiting convicted prisoners for 50 years and had infinitely more experience than I of exposure to deplorable human behaviour. His most notorious convicts were the Moors Murderers, Ian Brady and Myra Hindley, a long acquaintance with whom has done nothing to defeat his belief in redemption.

To close, I revert to Nilsen with an article written some six years after the first one. Although composed in tabloid style, it purports to describe the man from the perspective of a visitor rather than that of the chronicler of his homicidal career, and therefore illustrates the extent to which my understanding of him had evolved. No longer satisfied with attempting to explain his conduct, I was concerned to portray the individual, in a few broad strokes, with ordinary faults and characteristics. I had come by now, more than ever, to see the desire to kill as just one facet of a murderer's personality, albeit the most dramatic, destructive and contemptible, and to hold out the possibility that the human being might still be discerned beyond the carnage. A compulsive liar will do great harm, an unfaithful husband will sew unhappiness, and yet it would be facile to consider either of them to be immutably fixed by the narrow definitions of "liar" and "philanderer". Human nature is more complex than that, and the murderer is no less complex than the rest of us.

A danger naturally inheres in this attitude as well, and there may well be some justification for the accusation that I sail perilously close to being blind to what is intolerable. The liberal point of view is not always an easy one to defend.

The killer I know

My first impression of Dennis Nilsen was disconcerting. He seemed cocky, far too relaxed and self-assured in the circumstances, arm flopped casually over the back of a chair as he conducted the interview in the presence of two prison officers. It looked as if he was enjoying his notoriety, and was proud of his ability to manage events to his liking.

Nilsen believes that he can redeem himself only by small acts of communion with his fellow men, inch by inch, for the rest of his life. Surprisingly, he was concerned lest I find a frank account of his homicidal career over four years "distressing". It was an odd word to use for someone whose lack of emotion and automatism were to be exposed in court.

He was worried lest I be repelled or nauseated by some of the details he would reveal to me, but he quoted George Dandin as his protection: *"Vous l'avez voulu."* In addition to the stream of letters, Nilsen continued his prison journal which amounted to more than 40 closely written pages each, with random reminiscences from his childhood, the army, his civil service career, and the circumstances surrounding the deaths of his victims, often with vivid, gruesome, dispassionate detail.

The question must arise: why did Nilsen wish to co-operate so fully? It cannot be fame he is after, as he knew perfectly well that notoriety would come to him whether he wanted it or not. Nor can it be that he wanted a "tame" author to present his case in a rosy light. In the first place, he has never sought to exonerate or excuse his acts, the defence of diminished responsibility being a legitimate recognition that they might derive from a disorder of personality, which is a different matter.

When questioned about the disposal of the dead bodies, Nilsen parts company from the rest of us in stark, chilling fashion. He has been taken aback by the revulsion he has aroused as a result of dissection and dismemberment, and has postulated that it betrays a warped morality. He feels guilt about the "theft of lives" and is in no doubt about the wickedness of murders, but one cannot hurt a corpse, he says.

He goes so far as to berate those people who enjoy discussing the case as being unhealthily morbid. "I am always surprised that anyone can be attracted by the macabre," he writes. "I believe they can identify with 'dark images and acts' and loathe anything which reminds them of this side of themselves. The usual reaction is a flood of popular self-righteous condemnation but a willingness to, with friends and acquaintances, talk over and over again the appropriate bits of the case." There is, to say the least, a weird irony in this reprimand.

One priority at least has been slipping back to place in his disordered mind. We heard in court that he had not seen his mother for ten years. I had been struck by his apparent indifference to the unimaginable suffering she must have endured in recent months. He referred to it only once. The day before the trial, when he had read Dr MacKeith's report on his psychiatric condition, and I was about to go to see his mother in Scotland to prepare her for the trial, the last question I put to him was: what did he want me to tell her? With MacKeith's diagnosis uppermost in his mind, he thought for a moment, then said: "Tell her that there *is* an explanation."

Two emotions dominated Nilsen when he was sentenced to life imprisonment at the Old Bailey on Friday – disappointment and relief. The disappointment was because he had not had a chance to address the court. "I rehearsed my speech of thanks for two days for nothing," he told me in the visiting room minutes after hearing the judge recommend that he spend at least 25 years in prison.

The relief was that it was all over. I said to Nilsen: "It's been a long haul, Des." Nilsen replied: "Yes, a long road since 1978."

Nilsen had been expecting the verdict. He had written to me earlier saying: "Well, that's all for now folks. I'll write again at least once before the man in the red wig and the red-coloured drag sends me down for the last time."

The Sunday Times, 6 November 1983.

Is evil contagious?

There is one powerful image of which I shall never rid myself. It is of Dennis Nilsen at breakfast in his attic flat in Cranley Gardens, buttering a slice of toast and pouring a cup of coffee, while beside him, a few inches away, is the head of a man simmering in a pot on the greasy stove.

I know it to be a reasonably accurate image, owing little to imaginative fancy, because I have seen the photographs taken by police immediately after Nilsen's arrest, and I know what the boiled head looked like. I had to see the photographs to remind myself what this man had done, and picture what he had lived with, if only because at his trial one expert psychiatrist had declared that Nilsen suffered from no disorder of the personality, lawyers had insisted upon his sanity, and I had come to know him well and feel at ease in his company.

The disparity between the man and his deeds was, and remains, deeply troubling. One could have spent an evening with him chatting amiably or disputatiously about this and that, without any suspicion that he would go home to a corpse sitting in an armchair in front of the television, a body from which he had first squeezed the life, then washed, dried, powdered, cared for with devastating tenderness.

Nilsen once wrote to me that no one was prepared to accept that he was an ordinary man who had come to an extraordinary and overwhelming conclusion. Well, I accept it, and find in that acceptance more, not less, terror. It would be comforting if evil were monstrous or recognisable, if we could spot it and hurl abuse at it safely. But when it is concealed in a man of intelligence and wit, one's anchor to reality is shaken.

To write a book about such a man forces a shift in moral perceptions. Nothing in my experience had prepared me for it, since the literary and historical biographies I had previously written carried their own distance and made objectivity a natural outcome.

Like many people, I read of Nilsen's arrest, almost exactly two years ago, and suspected there was something unusual about the case which merited more than legal investigation. Naively and simply, I wrote to him in Brixton Prison.

This was not cunning, but common sense. To understand the mind of a murderer one would need written and verbal manifestation of how that mind worked. A regurgitation of newspaper reports would hardly suffice.

Correspondence between us developed into a torrent. Every day for eight months Nilsen wrote me a four-page letter, and in addition filled 50 prison exercise books with random reminiscences and reflections which he gave to his solicitor with instructions they should be passed to me after the trial.

Nilsen never asked for any benefit and made it clear from the beginning that he would not seek to interfer with what I was writing. I was free to draw my own conclusions and make my own assessments (his words), and he well knew that these were unlikely to be favourable. He did not want excuses or exoneration, merely cogent explanation which might be useful to others. He also quite openly enjoyed the attention, and I was always aware of the danger of serving his purposes.

There was another, more subtle, danger which directly affected the jumble of my own morality. My determination to understand how such a catastrophe was possible inevitably meant my trying to picture events from within Nilsen rather than describing them from outside. This required an effort of identification which was pregnant with peril.

More than this, there was always lurking the possibility of contamination. I do not pretend to know how evil operates or how one fends it off. I even distrust the word, and was surprised the judge at Nilsen's trial should use it. But most of us do not come into contact with a man who has done what Nilsen has done, and perhaps my work on the case might leave some mark.

He finally handed over to me what remained of his possessions, so that the contents of his flat (apart from items exhibited in evidence) were delivered to my doorstep. They included his television set, cassette-radio, correspondence files, some clothing, kitchen equipment, a home movie, the lighter and cigarette case presented to him by colleagues at the Jobcentre, and so on.

Could the proximity of these objects exert some fearful influence? The idea seemed preposterous, yet the reaction of some of my friends proved that it touched a chord somewhere beyond logic. My doctor cannot bear to talk about the subject, so uneasy does it make him. A well-known actress, whose life is bent upon the encouragement of goodness, worries about my moral safety.

I respect these views (or feelings), but contend that the two years I have spent on the book, ruminating on the subject for at least part of every day, has proven them wrong. Far from being morally confused, I have looked with acuity upon problems which never before exercised me, and they now stand forth in greater clarity.

Attendant burdens were far less easy to withstand. It was not pleasant to make my house burglar-proof as a precaution against interest from news-gatherers.

Nor did I welcome the odd telephone call from deranged persons warning me to stop work or else. I was appalled by the arrogant assumption that to write a study of a wilful murderer one had necessarily to be indifferent to the sufferings of victims' families. I still have to cope with this.

Nilsen remains an enigma. Contrary to stories invented by the worst of our newspapers, he is gregarious and chummy in prison; I have letters from other prisoners, since released, thanking him for his morale-boosting company. He reads voraciously and works well.

He also expects the sentence of the court to be applied, and not substituted by a harsher one decreed by the "screws", not because it matters what happens to him, but because the dispensers of justice should not have their roles usurped. He knows that his crimes are unpardonable; in quiet moments he can look upon the past with horror, yet at the same time talk with chilling detachment of the weight of a severed head.

As for me, I have learnt to be more cautious about the horizons of human behaviour and less tolerant of fantasy. I used to think individual fantasies were harmless, even beneficent and cathartic. I now know them to carry the seed of terrifying danger.

In my book I attempt to chart the course of Dennis Nilsen's fantasy life, which developed alongside his outwardly decent professional life for 15 years before it exploded into reality. An ordinary mirror fetish became mixed with a fascination for the idea of death, and the two gradually stretched into a kind of necrophilia, not as it is widely understood, which is gruesome enough, but more bizarrely a liking for the image of death and a feeling of warmth (!) in the propinquity of a corpse.

The source of Nilsen's aberration is, of course, a disorder of the personality, but that is hardly adequate. He is only an extreme instance of the rest of us, not a monster apart. Except at the time of murder, he retained his moral being.

A psychopath, we are told, has no concept of right and wrong, no understanding that his acts are bad. Nilsen is not psychopathic. He is lucid and cogent. He even courts the idea of punishment (it was he, after all, who wrote the letter to the landlords complaining that the lavatories were blocked, thus bringing plumbers and arrest within days).

The Devil does not waste his time corrupting the already corrupt; therein lies small victory. The Devil's greatest achievement is to twist a man with moral grasp into a man bereft, as Wringhim was twisted in James Hogg's masterpiece, *Confessions of a Justified Sinner*.

The Devil? You can call him "personality disorder" or "chemical imbalance in the body" or what you will. If a personality has been disordered by something, the implication is that it was once in good order. That should make each of us apprehensive.

The Observer, 10 March 1985.

Conversation between the author and Lord Longford on the nature of redemption

Masters: My experience with Nilsen has obliged me to consider aspects of human behaviour which most of us are able to keep at a safe distance. Having to deal with someone like him focuses one's moral perceptions more clearly and forces one to contemplate evil and decide what to do about it.

Longford: I would be very careful about the notion of evil. The formula is to hate the sin and love the sinner, which is, of course, very difficult. One has to loathe what such people do, not what they are, because human personality is sacred even though human behaviour is very often appalling. I would certainly not say that a person has been "taken over" by evil forces, only that he has done evil things. Take Sutcliffe, for instance, the Yorkshire Ripper. I went to see him last week. He thinks he has been taken over. He heard voices. He still does. But he used to think they were voices from God, and now he thinks they are from the Devil.

Masters: Is there a difference?

Longford: The voices are the same, but now he thinks he shouldn't obey them, and he's much happier. If you stick to saying "he's done evil things", rather than "he's an evil man", you can treat him as a human being. I remember Goddard (the late Lord of Appeal, Lord Goddard of Aldbourne) saying with tremendous gusto in the House of Lords years ago, during a debate on capital punishment, that "such a man should be destroyed". That kind of statement repels me.

Masters: It would me, too. But I am prepared to wonder if such people should not be avoided. Do you not think evil can be contagious?

Longford: I think it can be.

Masters: But haven't you run the risk?

Longford: Well, I haven't been exposed to it anything like as much as I would have done had I been working in a prison, for instance. I do think prisoners are contaminated by each other. But I haven't come anything close enough. My visits are only for an hour or so, and I have a family to come back to, and a whole life in the House of Lords. And I could be regarded as a puritanical person. I can't see myself as dangerously exposed, because I am subject to many more and much stronger influences. But you have been much closer to Nilsen than I ever was to Brady or Myra. You have become a kind of confessor.

Masters: I always thought understanding was essentially beneficent, that only good could come from it, but now I am not so sure. Can one understand too much or too deeply? If one can understand how and why someone might commit cruel murder, is there not a risk of complicity?

Longford: Theoretically. *Tout comprendre, c'est tout pardonner.* I can see that if you understood Nilsen you would be accused of being "soft on crime". Does it make you soft on crime if you sympathise too much?

Masters: Not soft on crime, but soft on punishment, perhaps. There are those who say that, in order to safeguard one's moral purity, one should resist understanding.

Longford: Rubbish! That's on the same level as people who say Myra Hindley ought to stay in prison in her own interest.

Masters: You have shown compassion for her, and have had to make yourself understand what she did, otherwise there would be no need to show compassion. Isn't there danger in that?

Longford: No. She was a perfectly normal girl before she met Brady and fell in love with him. She was simply infatuated. Quite early in the day, afterwards, she shook the whole thing off. She's never shown the slightest violence since the day she went to prison. She's been under observation for

25 years, and there's nothing violent in her character.

Masters: What about Brady? Did you make yourself understand what he did?

Longford: Not really, no. You would have to call him mental. He had hallucinations. Used to think the Home Office was pumping garbage into his cell.

Masters: Well, if you don't understand the crime, does that make forgiveness easier?

Longford: Oh, everybody's forgivable.

Masters: Even when, knowing what is morally good, they choose to do something morally bad?

Longford: I don't find any difficulty with that. It's the basis of Christianity. Forgive us our trespasses as we forgive those who trespass against us.

Masters: As long as they show contrition.

Longford: Even without contrition. You must forgive people who don't repent. It's impossible, anyway, to know whether anyone has repented or not. They may say they have, but who knows?

Masters: The public is much less ready to forgive, and sometimes chides you for it. You know that.

Longford: Yes, but people ignore the fact that I am naturally a rather disapproving person, and also that I firmly adhere to the principle of punishment. What I do not like is a punitive attitude. Punishment means controlling a punitive attitude and using it for Christian ends. Punishment ought to be a healing agent.

Masters: Many people would go further. They want to show their contempt. Have you never felt contempt for anyone?

Longford: Well, I would like to think not, but I'm sure I have. It's a weakness on my part. I don't pretend I live up to my own principles. That would be humbug. Part of growing older is that you are less ready to despise.

Masters: But do you despise Ian Brady?

Longford: I think it's very wrong to despise anybody. I

don't see it that way. What some people do might disgust me, but you have got to focus on the person.

Masters: Do you feel that you and Brady have anything in common?

Longford: We have everything in common. We're human beings. That's what I feel about everybody. And if I didn't feel it, I would go and confess.

Masters: But surely Brady was completely devoid of moral perception?

Longford: Well, I didn't know him until two or three years after the crimes. Here was a boy from the slums, with no schoolmaster or anybody who took an interest in him, yet, do you know, by the time I knew him he had a thorough knowledge of Tolstoy and Dostoevsky, he really was interested in the moral elements; that appealed to him. When Judgment comes, in view of Ian Brady's background, and taking into account all my advantages, will St Peter say to me, you've got to occupy a lower place than Brady? I don't know. I don't know what the calculation will be.

Masters: Do you mean that the difference between you is only of degree, not of kind? Somebody has stolen life from another, but is not essentially different from yourself?

Longford: No.

Masters: Have you done wicked things?

Longford: Wicked things? Not really. Cowardly things, no doubt. But I don't believe in goodies and baddies – that human beings are divided in that way.

Masters: So we can't make the distinction between good human beings and wicked human beings?

Longford: Not really. In practice, of course, some people are saints and others pretty awful . . .

Masters: So there are goodies and baddies.

Longford: In a way, and in another way not. There must be differences, but I don't feel it is right to make the distinction. A judge in court has to, of course . . . in the end there's a paradox.

Masters: Is Myra Hindley wicked?

Longford: Not now. I cannot think of two people more unlike than Brady and Myra. He's a mental case. He's much more to blame than she is. For good or ill, you can blame a person more if they're well balanced, I know, but there's no question that Myra's not mad. People who have never set eyes on her say all sorts of things about her. But those who have met her share my view that she's an honest woman. She's really very delightful.

Masters: Does she feel guilty?

Longford: You can't say really. I suppose a Catholic has an easier time, he can go to confession. Does Nilsen still feel guilty?

Masters: He did, but he says if he were to go on feeling guilty he would go out of his mind.

Longford: Perfectly true.

Masters: But surely we demand that they should go on feeling guilty, that they accept responsibility. Nilsen recognises his guilt, but probably doesn't feel is so much now. Yet if he and Brady are to have ultimate blame excused by childhood influences and the like, then where is the notion of Free Will? You can undermine that notion with explanations of heredity or environment or chemical imbalances in the brain. It is tantamount to saying the killer did not have a choice. Did Brady have a choice?

Longford: Oh yes, he had a choice. There is no sin without Free Will. But I think you get into a difficult area here. You can't say that all people who are mentally ill are not responsible, that Ronnie Kray is less to blame than Reggie Kray, for instance. There must be a question of degree somewhere. How you should punish people when there is a mental factor at work is not easy . . .

Masters: But it's of fundamental importance, it seems to me, to a Christian. If somebody is mentally deficient and therefore not entirely aware of what he is doing, he is not exercising Free Will: his Will is imprisoned, he has no control over it, he is simply not free at all. Thus the whole idea of psychiatric excuses undermines that Christian doctrine.

Longford: There are Christian psychiatrists, you know.

Masters: One of the psychiatrists at his trial said Nilsen wasn't insane, he just liked killing people. I don't suppose he was a Christian.

Longford: Well, what do you think?

Masters: You cannot butter a slice of toast while a few inches away there simmers the head of somebody you have known, eat the toast and still be sane.

Longford: What ought to be done with Nilsen, then?

Masters: I think he ought to be studied and treated, as much for our sake as for his. There ought to be some continuing attempt to make him better understand the inadmissibility of his acts, as apparently Myra now does. And we ought to be able to work out what makes a person like him descend into that particular hell. It's a kind of duty.

Longford: Talking to you was obviously a sort of exorcism.

Masters: But that's not enough. It's bad enough for me, but I know people out there want retribution, not healing. All those millions who would like to see a return of hanging, *Sun* readers and hell-raisers at Conservative conferences, do they have moral perceptions, or do they not?

Longford: On public issues people's views are much less worthwhile than on something they know about. You cannot pretend that the opinion of the man in the street on, say, what should have been done in Iraq, is really of much value.

Masters: But on a penal issue?

Longford: They haven't studied the question at all. They're not even aware that hanging's not a deterrent. They know nothing about it whatever.

Masters: About the usefulness of deterrence, no, but on the moral grounds that surely is unnecessary. Either you have a conscience or you don't.

Longford: I don't think so. The ordinary opinion of the man in the street is of no value in that context.

Masters: He can have no moral judgment?

Longford: If he's sensible he won't pretend to an opinion on a large moral issue if the facts have not been presented to him.

Masters: He may instinctively feel that it's morally correct for a murderer to be hanged.

Longford: A thing like that can not be determined by instinct.

Masters: If a moral view is not determined by instinct, then what is it determined by? Ethologists have traced the origins of our morality in patterns of animal behaviour, which have evolved into our inhibitions and conscience.

Longford: I don't pay the slightest attention to that. No one in Parliament would pay attention to any view based on what ethologists say. 2,000 years of Christianity . . .

Masters: Christianity surely trusts the man in the street to have a valid moral view.

Longford: About his personal behaviour, yes, matters within his sphere, but not on public issues. He hasn't studied his subject.

Masters: Well, you have studied all aspects of penal reform in a long life. The worry still persists that perhaps, when we meet murderers like Brady and Nilsen, that we are deceived by them. I have heard it suggested that you are naive. Could the Devil be working through these people?

Longford: He might be, but I don't think it matters much.

Masters: It matters if he succeeds.

Longford: I don't believe in a personal Devil, anyway. What matters is the constant possibility of redemption. And we must always be ready to make allowances. Let me tell you of an interesting case. A young woman killed her mother with a hammer and went to prison on a life sentence. She came out after two-and-a-half years because it was realised she had been suffering from a combination of post-natal depression and pre-menstrual tension. Now she's leading a perfectly sensible and useful life. The general view was, you couldn't totally blame her in the circumstances. You can't ignore things like that. It gives us hope.

The Sunday Telegraph, 19 May 1991.

Nilsen since conviction

Since conviction, Nilsen has been to Wormwood Scrubs, Parkhurst, Wakefield, Full Sutton, Yorkshire, Parkhurst again, and now Her Majesty's Prison Albany, on the Isle of Wight.

During that time I have been visiting him regularly, weekly as the trial approached, and since his dispersal to distant British Rail destinations, about once every six weeks.

When I wrote the book on his case, my subject was a murderer and my study was precisely focused, detached and analytical.

That was many years ago. This is how Dennis Nilsen appears to me now. He is tall, thin, a little stooped and round-shouldered. Now 46, he shows no sign of balding and has few grey hairs. His voice retains traces of a Scottish accent (he was born in Fraserburgh, at the north-east tip of Aberdeenshire), and his manner is infectiously cheerful.

In fact, it is his sense of humour which comes as the biggest shock, as if someone who has done what he has done should not be allowed the luxury of laughter.

Sometimes his sharpness is enviable. We were once talking of lawyers who feign an interest in a case merely to stretch it out and earn more in legal aid. "I know what you mean," said Nilsen. "The sort of man who has a tax-deductible heart."

Earlier instances of wisecracks, the sort that would not shame a stand-up comic, have found their way into the press over the years and have confirmed his reputation as a man bereft of emotion.

To joke about the cast of a film being given "in order of disappearance" is ugly.

Yet this reputation is short-sighted. Nilsen has his emotions; I have seen him angry, indignant, ashamed, grateful, bitter, enthusiastic and depressed. Never, I must say, resigned.

He knows full well that he will never be at liberty and does not hanker after it. He realises he deserves the fate which the court has decreed.

But he resists being diminished still further by the system, being robbed of the right to any independent decision, that state of numbered non-being to which some prisoners are reduced.

Even your bowels must obey prison rules. So Nilsen sometimes suffers for suggesting that prison rules are broken by warders and governors as well as convicts and he has spent several sessions on the punishment block as a result.

The authorities regard him as a trouble-maker. He regards himself as holding on to some individuality.

"You must instinctively distrust all organised power," he says.

"The power of the mob is as often to be seen in government as on the street.

"They will treat you like a pawn on a chessboard if they can."

He always has a cell to himself, from which he is let out for work or exercise. When not "down the block" (on punishment) he reads two or three books a week, usually historical or biographical, composes music on an electronic keyboard which he received as a gift a year ago, and writes.

He has recently written an essay on Mussolini, with source references, for a history lecturer who comes in once a week. It is a competent piece of work. He has also done some painting.

I have often noticed in conversation that Nilsen is so intent on what he is saying, so bent upon making his point of view known, that he does not actually listen.

As I am talking, I can watch the thoughts go through his mind as he forms the words of his next declamation. There is a kind of obsession about his need to convince, and a kind of fear in his reluctance to be convinced by anyone else.

We do not, of course, talk about murder all the time, but range over world events, British politics, films and books, gossip and history.

It is usually he, however, who introduces the subject. When I do, I find it is quickly submerged by something else.

Contrary to popular prejudice, Nilsen is not despised or feared by other convicts. I have seen them talk with him in the normal spirit of camaraderie one would expect in prison conditions.

Besides which, he is on a wing where everyone has done something pretty awful, which rather lessens his "monstrosity".

He refers to the "myth" of Nilsen the Monster as some confection of the tabloid press, as if he had not, in fact, squeezed the life from up to 15 people and mutilated their bodies.

He knows these were monstrous acts and talks of "the regressive personality" who was responsible for them, but would dearly like to place all that behind him and look to the future.

His biggest quarrel with me arose because my book

concentrated on the past and would not finish on a note of optimism, of rehabilitation, of self-renewal.

"You must never succumb to the urge to put men in neat traditional pigeon-holes," he chided.

"I am always learning towards self-definition. God has still refused to declare his existence, British politics is still as disreputable as ever, and the police are still the largest criminal organisation on these islands."

Some of this is said with a view to shock, the underlying motive of many a radical. But much of it derives from experience in the army, the police force and the civil service before his conviction. And in prison since.

He insists on loyalty to belief as well as to individuals. He does not say or do anything which might compromise another con and is eager to subscribe to the convention that you do not "grass" on inmates.

Nevertheless, and despite his being no friend of the warders, I have known him refuse to take sides against a prison warder in a dispute if he *knows* him to be the injured party.

"You must stand up for the truth wherever you see it," he says.

Nilsen does not take himself seriously as a potent figure of modern legend. He refuses to answer letters from crackpots. "Do they think I'm some kind of mystical guru?" he asks.

He was appalled to hear that a schoolboy had pictures of him covering the walls of his bedroom.

He read *The Silence of the Lambs*, though he has obviously not seen the film. Video films are available in a communal room once a week but he says they rarely venture above the level of *Mary Poppins*.

"The Hannibal Lecter character is a fraudulent fiction," Nilsen insists. "Nobody does what he is supposed to have done through power and control. My offences were committed precisely because I never had any power in my life.

"They are the acts of weak men, not impressively intelligent characters. Lecter is invented to titillate the public, not to give any idea of truth."

He knows that I have made, and will make, no excuses for his offences. Still, I freely admit that my two hours in the visiting room with Dennis Nilsen are often stimulating, sometimes amusing, and never boring.

I do not remind myself all the time that I am sitting opposite a murderer. I take a packet of cigarettes and we drink our way through several cups of coffee.

He has a cell to himself because the prison decided he needed protecting and shares it with his eight-year-old budgerigar, Hamish.

"Hamish" was named rather prematurely and turned out to be a girl.

"When I have a meal she arrives on my shoulder and I have to feed her a few morsels direct from my mouth. It's part of the bonding ritual, you know.

"A budgie doesn't live eight years unless it is happy."

It is ironic that such a remark should come from a man whose social bonds were so fragile, so thread-like, that his personality disintegrated under the pressure of isolation and he became known only for his crimes as a multiple killer.

It makes one wonder just how frail is anyone's grip on his own mysterious psyche.

The Sunday Express, 5 January 1992.

CHAPTER 2

The Addictive Killer

Until the 1980s, killers who claimed more than one or two victims were generally referred to as "mass murderers". As public interest in the phenomenon grew, however, it was perceived that this appellation ought strictly to apply only to those killers who, in an access of rage or bitterness, turn their derangement upon the anonymous folk who happen to surround them at any one moment. Such was the case with James Huberty at McDonald's restaurant in San Diego, California, on 18 July 1984. He opened fire at random on a routine day in an ordinary place and massacred 21 persons, mostly children. He was said to be frustrated by lack of advancement in his work, and had told his wife he was going out hunting. Similarly, on 1 August 1966, Charles Whitman had climbed the tower at the University of Texas campus in Austin, and spent one and a half hours sniping at ant-like creatures far below, scattering in panic. He killed 14 and wounded another 30. He, too, was fed up with life, it seems. We cannot know what possessed Michael Ryan to gun down 15 strangers at lunchtime as he meandered through the streets of Hungerford on 19 August 1987, because he committed suicide without explaining himself. But his actions were not incompatible with the pattern of morosity, sullenness, low achievement and sudden explosion of tight, concentrated fury displayed by Huberty and Whitman. All three of them may be said to have run "amok" (the word is Malay for "homicidal assault") to impress the world, once and once only, with the previously unnoticed fact of their existence; they truly murdered in the mass.

People like Nilsen are no longer referred to as mass murderers but as "serial killers", because their victims are slain separately, one by one, over a long period of time. The other stark difference is, of course, that the murders are secret, private, concealed events, not a public display of self. There have been many cases in history, from Gilles de Rais to Lacenaire to Jack the Ripper, but the increased frequency of this kind of crime in recent years has caused considerable alarm. The names of Theodore Bundy, John Wayne Gacy, Dean Coril, Peter Sutcliffe (the so-called "Yorkshire Ripper"), strike fear into the heart, for they are somewhere among us, unseen and unsuspected. They use the same shops and catch the same buses and appear in every sense normal. But their subterranean lives are a florid expression of Hell, and the damage they wreak is a repellent blot upon human nature.

The term "serial" killer is, I think, a misnomer, for it posits a plan of long-term intention which is unlikely. These people do not establish in advance a design to commit a "series" of crimes, but rather lurch from one to the next in a haphazard, unpremeditated flounder. (I do not mean to suggest that each crime is unpremeditated – on the contrary, it usually shows signs of careful preparation – but that the personality change, or "mood", which precedes the preparation of the crime and makes it possible, is unpremeditated. "Each one was its own last time," said Nilsen of his murders.) More apposite would be "repetitive killer", or even better, "addictive killer", as there is some evidence that this kind of murder is akin to an addiction.

Often presaged by many years of fantasising, the first murder is an acutely shocking event to the murderer, who can scarcely believe what he has done, expects arrest at any moment, and is frantic to rid himself of the evidence of his conduct. This is not to say that he derived no enjoyment from the act (he would hardly do it if it gave him *dis*pleasure), but that he retains enough moral sense to know that he should not derive such pleasure. The day fantasy breaks free of its restrictive frontier and tumbles over into reality is the beginning of the addiction, the first "fix". After that, the murderer tries to resist, to control his monstrous craving; one year elapsed between Nilsen's first crime and his second, and an astonishing nine years separated Jeffrey Dahmer's first and second murders. Dahmer referred to the first as his "sin".

With the second death, the addictive killer knows that he is not strong enough to withstand the pressures of the need (though he still hopes he might), and the murders rush into a spiral of madness. Nilsen killed three people in the last two months before his arrest, and by the time Dahmer was caught, he had an apartment littered with human debris, having murdered six men in the preceding seven weeks. The addiction always wins in the end.

The addictive killer is a more interesting phenomenon than the mass murderer, for he opens a window on to the nature of evil, its insinuation into the personality, and its periodic banishment therefrom. The "good" individual and his "bad" inner self exist both simultaneously and sequentially, the one not interfering with the other.

The first article in this chapter considers this primitive Manichaeism in the addictive killer and tentatively introduces the use of religious language. It is interesting to me that the religious viewpoint was of little consequence, as far as I was concerned, until I began to ruminate upon murder. It is through the contemplation of murder that I have come to realise that the Devil (for want of a better word) can only triumph over goodness – there must be something there for him to fight. To infect an already amoral or immoral person would be a hollow victory indeed. Thus the mass murderers are bereft of moral scruple (they have gone berserk and are not moral beings at all), and the addictive murderers are all too well aware, in the periods between killings, how wicked they have been and may still be. Theirs is a struggle, which both they and their victims lose.

The second article was published the week after Dahmer was arrested in 1991, but it is general in scope. I wanted to indicate what characteristics such killers may have in common, which would enable them to be recognised in advance of their descent into crime. This is somewhat akin to a new science called "profiling", but only tangentially. The profiler will assist the police in their search for an unknown murderer by putting together the circumstances and nature of the crime, the method and habits of the criminal, in order to build a picture of the kind of man he might be. My list of characteristics (based upon various scientific studies) is meant to be pre-emptive, and it concentrates on the personality of the necrophile. I have since disowned the final word in this piece, and agree with Lord Longford that nobody is irredeemable, though there are many who have done nothing yet to redeem themselves.

There follow two book reviews, one examining the thesis of Mary Midgley – that wickedness derives from intellectual laziness (*not* thinking too precisely on the event) – and the other looking at the idea that murder is a work of art; this demonstrates to what absurdities too much theorising may lead.

The killer comes into his own

In his summing up for the jury at the trial of mass murderer Dennis Nilsen in 1983, Mr Justice Croom-Johnson said: "There are evil people who do evil things. Committing murder is one of them." He warned the jurors that there should be no excuses for moral defects or a nasty nature.

To the judge, evil was an adjective describing behaviour which departed from the norm and could be viewed objectively, from a distance. There was no metaphysical confusion about this, no questioning or pondering the concept of evil as noun, as a thing which exists eternally and must eternally be fought by all of us.

Murderers are our salvation. They enable us to feel good about ourselves, because we could not possibly be so horrible as they.

The whole of Germany relished the case of Peter Kürten in the 1930s. No one could be more "evil" than a man who confessed to glorying in the sight, smell and taste of blood and looked forward to his own execution when he would feel his own blood gush forth; who, at the age of nine, had pushed little boys into the Rhine and who, by the time he was 13 was stabbing sheep as he sodomised them.

Kürten murdered something over 20 people in a fury of sadistic lust, and when there were no human victims available, he would stop in the park, break the neck of a swan and drink the blood. A psychiatrist, one Dr Berg, declared that Kürten was sane (two psychiatrists testified to the sanity of Nilsen). He was just different.

The point is that Kürten's loathsome conduct was human, not *in*human; it is only our own species which can refine cruelty to such a grotesque degree, which is why the Christian religion teaches that we are intolerably tainted. The potential for good and evil is within all of us, and it is instructive to find that many serial murderers talk in "dualistic" terms, referring to the forces of dark and light that alternately possess them.

Nilsen called himself "monochrome man", all black and white, and one of his intended victims, whom he tried to throttle and drown before carefully reviving over a period of 36 hours, said that Nilsen had behaved like a saint both before and after his murderous attack, when he seemed "something else". Nilsen wrote in his prison journal: "I ignored my demons for years; they sprung out and destroyed me."

There are many other examples of murderers who illustrate the primitive religious principle of man's dualistic condition. Women in Jersey were terrorised for 11 years my a vicious rapist on the island. When he was caught, he turned out to be Edward Paisnel, a man whom dozens of children referred to as "Uncle Ted", a benign and friendly soul and a regular Santa Claus at Christmas. Paisnel said he thought he was periodically possessed by a demon. Ed Gein was a popular and reliable baby-sitter in Wisconsin. He also murdered women and ate parts of their bodies.

St Augustine thought that evil was a perverseness of the will, and it is certainly true that the will is at its strongest when in the grip of a murderous desire to cause destruction. It then becomes indifferent to the pain it inflicts, horrifyingly detached. Goodness is a much humbler, gentler force, and much more enduring. Evil must take advantage of a weakening of the personality in order to take hold, and its dominance is shortlived, until the power of good reasserts itself.

Nilsen said he was astonished at the strength that surged through his body when he was in the throes of the act of murder, as if another force was using him and inhabiting him temporarily.

It follows that those murderers who are the most diabolically possessed are those, paradoxically, who retain some moral sense. Evil has no victory unless there is some good to conquer. Hence, those psychopaths who cannot distinguish between right and wrong, who do wrong without knowing it, cannot really have evil in them. They are banal and unenlightening, sowing terror from a moral chaos.

On the other hand, murderers who know their acts to be wrong, yet still choose to do them, are witness to the power of evil at its most intense. They are not different from us, but extreme examples of us, as we are all fallible enough to do wrong when we know we should do right.

There are some philosophers who suggest that murder is a creative act, a means whereby something worse, like a meltdown of the soul, is prevented. A lot of the time, Dennis Nilsen seemed to be struggling to avoid self-disintegration, and yet it is interesting that he engineered, to some extent, his own discovery and arrest. He had seen evil at its closest, and had been its servant. Yet he still recognised it for what it was.

Evil's final triumph comes with the need for punishment. Were the murderer to collapse into regrets and remorse, the manic power would have wasted its time. Its design is fulfilled with the desire for punishment, which implicitly celebrates its success.

The Sunday Telegraph, 17 February 1991.

What makes a monster?

When police officers entered the flat of Jeffrey Dahmer in Milwaukee last week, they came upon a scene so intensely squalid and nauseating as to paralyse the imagination. They are, apparently, still reeling from the shock of finding heads in the fridge and assorted genitalia in bottles, and cannot begin to grasp, by an analogy drawn from experience or observation, how it is possible for a man to live surrounded by the debris of dismembered bodies yet still appear banal and ordinary.

Surely if a personality disintegrates in such a bizarre and spectacular fashion, it ought to give out some overt

signs to alert the rest of us to the danger of imminent
collapse, some small eloquent echoes of the turmoil within.
The idea that a monster may exist among us unrecognised
is frankly unbearable. It is also unscientific.

Though our knowledge is still somewhat tentative, a
number of studies into the psychology of multiple murder,
or serial killing, have been undertaken since the war, and
it is possible to compose a portrait of the type of person
whose symptoms might explode into full-blown homicidal
necrophilia. The trouble is, the symptoms are innocuous
when considered in isolation, and may well apply to a
great many healthy people. It is their confluence and col-
lision which cause the triumph of impulse over restraint. In
Dahmer's case it is particularly worrying that there seems
to have been an opportunity to prevent the tragedy.

A year ago he was released from prison after serving time
for molesting an adolescent boy, whom he had sought to
photograph naked. In this alone lie two important signs.
As Dr Robert Brittain demonstrated in his exhaustive study
of motiveless murder 21 years ago, most multiple killers
start with a minor sexual offence the importance of which
is not acknowledged at the time, and most are fascinated
by photography, indeed consumed by the need to take
pictures. Dennis Nilsen, who like Dahmer dismembered his
corpses and boiled the heads, cherished his movie camera
and was obsessed by the desire to create images. Apparently
Dahmer's cupboards were crammed with snapshots of his
victims, taken both when alive and at various stages of
dismemberment.

Other significant characteristics of the potential serial
murder are a withdrawn, introspective nature given to
solitary pleasures, shyness, severe isolation, and the ability
to communicate without fear of humiliation. Dean Coril,
the Houston mass murderer of the seventies, was hypersen-
sitive, morose, and unsociable. Nilsen was described as
an inveterate "loner". Dahmer's former schoolfriends have

already pointed out that he was left very much to himself.

Our putative serial killer might also be prissily protective about his health, even to the point of hypochondria. He is also likely to be latently homosexual, but with very limited and never satisfactory experience, and emotionally impoverished. He is chronically unable to judge the motives of others, and therefore will always appear distrustful and "chippy". He is under 35, narcissistic, vain, intelligent, and pedantic about details.

Peter Kürten, the Düsseldorf sadist, had precise recall of murders he had committed 30 years before, down to exact addresses and times. Method dominates the murderer's daily routine. He is morbidly vulnerable and deeply resentful of innocent criticism. His compensatory drive for power and superiority is consequently disproportionate and ought to be noticeable to a trained eye. He finds it difficult to be aggressive without being destructive, and he may have a history of fire-raising.

It seems that Dahmer's father spotted that his son was heading for disaster, and pleaded with the probationary service to give him some psychiatric care as a "last chance". Yet the probation officer did not visit him, and so the chance was neglected. Had he succeeded in knowing young Dahmer reasonably well, he might also have detected the aberrant characteristics of an incipient necrophile, as enumerated by Erich Fromm.

Those include the habit of breaking matchsticks in half, a tendency to featureless, lifeless conversation, a pallid visage, a predilection for monochrome rather than colour, and especially a fascination with things mechanical. Peter Sutcliffe, the Yorkshire Ripper, knew as much about engines as he did about the habits of Northern prostitutes.

In the last analysis, however, there is one overriding defect of personality shared by all mass murderers which it is impossible to discern in advance, and that is a rich, overblown fantasy life which must, by definition, be secret.

There is nothing inherently wrong or abnormal about fantasy. In a child it is a proper stage in the taming and befriending of an otherwise possibly hostile universe. The cinema, in which everyone is famous, beautiful and popular, later encourages fantasy life, and most of us retain into adulthood some private fantasies which we use as instruments to mitigate a problem in real life, if not to solve it. In fantasy, we are our director, actor and cameraman, and the denouement is guaranteed to satisfy.

The danger arises when the boundaries between fantasy and reality break down, when fantasy life is cherished so lovingly that the subject's hold on reality evaporates. This is demonstrably what happened to Dennis Nilsen who, once his fantasies had been enacted, yearned to repeat them. "I caused dreams which caused death," he wrote. "This is my crime." And again, "I killed those men in order to create the best image of them," once more insisting upon a perverse ideal which far outranks drab reality.

How any probation officer can be expected to watch a mind grow so distorted as to require eventual nourishment in death, it is difficult to see. It is only when it is too late that fantasy becomes visible, by which time real people have been cast in the role of "props" and have no function outside the murderer's diseased imagination. This must certainly have occurred in Milwaukee, or the "real" Jeffrey Dahmer could not have continued living surrounded by fragments of limbs and putrescence without going mad.

All multiple killers speak of the regret they feel at the distress they have caused, but do not equate this with remorse, because they were compelled to respond to an irresistible stimulus. They claim they have no control, that when the urge to create death possesses them, nothing on earth can stop the terrible scene from taking place.

Forbes in Australia, Heirens in Illinois, Christie in London, all testify to being deserted by the inhibitory factor of moral control at the time of killing. The pressure to do something is overwhelming. "The loner has to achieve fulfilment alone within himself," wrote Dennis Nilsen. "All he has are his own extreme acts. People are merely supplementary to the achievement of these acts. He is abnormal and he knows it."

Murder is sometimes a way of preventing something worse from happening (to the ego, that is), such as a detonation or imploding of violent impulses. The murderer often sees himself as victim *manqué*, and would dearly love to swap places with the poor creature he has killed. Necrophilia, says Ernest Jones, is the extreme perversion of the love instinct. On the other hand, Fromm sees the necrophile as the ultimate narcissist, whose enemy is life itself.

It is indeed tragic that these signs of alarm go undetected, for with trained attention to the clues which may be strewn, and a determined professional desire to prevent serial murder rather than just record it after the event, the horrors that were revealed in Milwaukee might have been avoided. At the very least, Dahmer's conviction on a charge of sexual molestation ought to have guaranteed that he was kept under close observation. He wasn't, and his flat became instead the florid expression of a mind so poisoned by fantasy as to be irredeemable.

The Sunday Telegraph, 28 July 1991.

Mary Midgley's philosophy of murder

Philosophers have an endearing habit of tackling problems they know to be insoluble, for the pleasure and instruction that can be derived from the effort. Mary Midgley has set herself the awesome task of working out why, when allowance has been made for external causes which make things go wrong in this world, there remains "a thumping residue of human conduct which seems quite unnecessarily bad". The enquiry takes her on a journey of such dense and allusive perception, via Socrates, Nietzsche, Freud and Lorenz, that I have now read the book twice, not because it is difficult (on the contrary, it reads with the ease and elegance of Bertrand Russell), but because it is so stimulating.

Mrs Midgley swiftly dispenses with a number of red herrings. To ascribe wicked behaviour to the pressures of "society" or to mental illness would be to deny ourselves the power of self-direction, to chuck away the map by which we direct ourselves. Nor is it true to say that the map has been invented and imposed from without; even the immoralists like Nietzsche, properly understood, accept the existence of our moral map but recommend alternative routes to be taken within it. Another nonsense is often heard in the mouths of those dogmatic sceptics who claim that no one has a right to judge anyone else, on the grounds that all moral decisions are private. This is impossible, because we can only make moral choices by comparing them with other choices made in the past, both by ourselves and by others, and assessing the benefit or error. One must not confuse moral misjudgment with the absence of moral judgment.

The capacity for moral choice is probably inherited from our animal ancestry, but it is a mistake to conclude, simply, that bad behaviour is due to the aggressive instinct. In the first place, aggression is a positive boon – children need it in order to develop sympathy; secondly, there are other parts of our inherited baggage which can prove just as sinister without the aid of aggression.

Away with excuses! Mary Midgley would have us honestly face that wrong doing is a property of humankind, something we will not get rid of. We can only alleviate its propensity to poison our affairs by understanding why it happens. Mrs Midgley's thesis is that each of us is engaged in a constant debate about what to do, and that one of the alternatives postulated by our internal lawyer is always to do something evil. This imperative is usually balanced in the conflict of motives by other considerations – selflessness, fear, love, what you will – and the resulting action manages to put the desire to do wrong in its place. Sometimes, however, one motive will urge itself with such force that it suppresses all others and the need to satisfy it becomes obsessive. Normal anger may harden into resentment, then hatred, then the compulsive wish to destroy. What allows this process is, in fact, intellectual laziness.

Morality has evolved, as Darwin recognised and Freud did not, from our own horror at the contemplation of our destructive motives. It is a means for arbitrating inner conflict by a system of priorities. But it needs constant thought, honesty and discernment. "The harm that can be done by not thinking is immeasurable," writes Mrs Midgley. Leaving aside for the moment the possible dissension of poor Hamlet, one must agree that the conclusion is correct, and not nearly as banal as it seems. Eichmann was evil literally through thoughtlessness, having successfully smothered his capacity to reflect upon what he was doing. Mary Midgley rightly points out that psychology is an art – it must be hauled out of the clumsy hands of doctors. If we practise it properly upon ourselves, we should end up doing the right thing. Some may even hone their intuitions to such an extent that they can write a book as richly interesting as this.

There is a snag, of course. Some intelligent men are capable of seeing all this and still choosing evil as a preference. To call such people psychopathic (as Midgley tends to by implication) is to avoid an unpleasant complication. Until he actually *does* something psychopathic, such a man is absolutely one of us.

The Spectator, 15 September 1984.

The aesthetics of murder

It has long been acknowledged that apparently motiveless murder defeats analysis or even understanding from both the legal and the moral standpoints. Joel Black now tells us why. It is because we have not been taking into account our own complicity as spectators. The only way to comprehend a pointless killing is to grasp it as a work of art; the murderer is the artist and we, the audience, are afforded the opportunity of a "peak aesthetic experience" in the contemplation of the crime.

Well, it is a novel approach, to say the least, and before it is dismissed as arrant nonsense, it should be allowed that Professor Black has written a stimulating and pregnant study on an unusual theme, richly allusive and fertilised by wise learning. We are taken through Kant to De Quincey and on to Chapman's slaying of John Lennon by way of Burke and Hare and De Palma's film, *Dressed to Kill*, as well as Camus, Marcel Schwob, Nietzsche, Hitchcock and Gide. It is quite a feast. The trouble is that one is left with the impression that if you ruminate on an idea long enough you can come up with all kinds of notions, especially when they are wrapped up in barely digestible academic jargon.

The affinity between art and murder, says Black, has been recognised by only a few artists and murderers; of the former, the most notable is De Quincey, who first proposed murder as an art form, and of the latter, the French killer Lacenaire (who thought himself a great poet, but whom Black regards as a great murderer) offers the best example. When murder is viewed from this angle, we do not have to understand it, which is impossible and therefore frustrating, but simply to enjoy it. An artistic murder cannot be a hot-blooded crime of passion, but must be a cold-blooded act in which jealousy and revenge play no part.

This leads to some dodgy reflections (i.e. that the murderer is a kind of Nietzschean superman, spared the banal constraints to which the non-artist is subject), and some logical acrobatics (i.e. that murder is a creative art because it is destructive). Most importantly, the meaningless murder, like an earthquake, is an expression of the sublime. "An event is sublime when its cause is hidden; it is absurd when it has no cause at all." Which is to beg the question, since if the cause is hidden, then there is no way of knowing whether it is there or not; one might as well say that what is apparently absurd is secretly sublime, which is obviously a *non sequitur*. Professor Black steers himself into these messes rather frequently.

The idea that gratuitous violence, or the *acte gratuit* devoid of purpose and indifferent to consequence, is sublime, is an extension of the Romantic impulse, and it is no surprise to learn that to reach this sublimity we are required to see the murder through the killer's eyes and not the victim's. Complicity is essential. The audience then collaborates in the depiction of violence as a fantasy in a frame – the image caught within that square of the cinema screen or the snapshot print. It is significant that many murderers feel the need to photograph their victims, and nourish ambitions to be film-directors; the "creative" act of murder cannot really exist until it has been recorded by the fantasy world – before that it is merely a brutal act of nastiness.

Which leads to Black's final thesis, that murder is encouraged by film and television, in so far as they blur distinctions between reality and fantasy and make it easier to see killing as an "artistic" event. Thus murder and acting are allied, and the murderer, deprived for whatever reason of an identity in the real world, claims one in the theatrical world of the captured image. When Hinckley tried to kill Mr Reagan, they both played their roles perfectly, but for one of them it was a début. And when Yukio Mishima killed himself he assumed the role of director as well.

This book can be recommended to those who like to thrash about odd conceits, but they must be warned that some of the language will hinder their progress – like trying to dance in treacle. Invented words ("victimage" and "celebricide") and squashed phrases ("hyperaestheticised mass-culture", "aristocratic-aesthetic hyperreality", and "mass-media-mediated fictions"), do rather make one sigh. There are some passages from which I could tease no meaning at all.

The Spectator, 14 December 1991.

CHAPTER 3

Victims

The necrophilous murderer may claim to have despatched his victim with as little pain as possible, and to have derived no pleasure from the act of killing – his pleasure was in the *result* of killing, that is the possession of a corpse. However, he remains cruelly indifferent to the devastation caused to those whose lives were in some way attached to his victim, or to those whose lives have been poisoned by contact with him, because he does not inhabit the same emotional world as they. It is impossible for him to experience the empathetic imagination which enables one to shed tears over the misfortunes of others. He simply does not *know* how they feel. He is bereft of sentiment. His selfishness is absolute.

The present chapter examines some of the manifold ways in which the destructiveness of the murderer affects many more than the individuals who died at his hands, his act of despoliation sending ripples of pain towards distant boundaries of which he is unaware. There is the long, desolate patience of the family of Fiona Jones in a foreign land, as they wait for news of their missing daughter, sister and wife, while police search for clues. They dare not think she has been murdered, but they know that the probabilities must point in that direction. I spent days with them in France and wrote the article before the case was solved. It was a vivid instance of the slow slaughter of hope and the anguish of impotent love faced with incomprehensible caprice. Fiona's buried remains were discovered some weeks later.

Secondly, there is the enduring suffering of Carl Stottor,
almost killed by Nilsen and subsequently spared. He is
alive, but severely damaged, his trust in tatters and his
moral compass knocked awry. Third, the sad digging
in a back garden in north London for possible victims
of a ring of murderous paedophiles, which not only
affected the families of missing children, but profoundly
depressed the man who led the enquiry, Detective Chief
Superintendent Roger Stoodley. Himself a family man, and
endowed with considerable tolerance, he eventually secured
some convictions, but knows that a principal villain has
still not been indicted. He devoted the closing years of
his career to this case, intent upon justice being served,
and has been left with an ineradicable sense of pity for
the helpless young of London.

The case of Simon Dale presents a different kind of
victim, that of the unassuaged dead. Slain in his home in
Shropshire, his ex-wife Baroness de Stempel was charged
with his murder and acquitted. She was found guilty of
other, related charges involving fraud and forgery, but no
charges of murder were brought against anyone else, and
the case remains unsolved. Other victims of this incident
are the friends and neighbours of the deceased, who felt
horrified indignation as Dale's character and reputation
were besmirched by evidence in court, and my article attempted to make their voices heard.

Finally, I have considered the different ways in which
the families of a murder victim may cope with tragedy
in the years that follow, from the implacable hatred of
Mrs West, mother of Lesley Ann Downey, to the tentative
forgiveness of Gordon Wilson, whose daughter died in the
Enniskillen bomb outrage. The burden of this article is to
explore the survival of the human spirit and its capacity to
resume a positive response to life after the cruel blow of a
brutal bereavement.

There are yet other casualties, rarely given a thought by

commentators, namely the families of the convicted murderer. I know that Mrs Scott, mother of Dennis Nilsen, and Dr Lionel Dahmer, father of Jeffrey Dahmer, have never recovered from the shock dealt to their quiet quotidian security by the acts of their offspring, but the public is little concerned with their pain. The finest account of such a relationship is by Mikal Gilmore, brother of Gary Gilmore who was executed by firing-squad in the United States in 1977. His reflections upon the fate his brother imposed upon his family are due to be published in 1994, and I commend them to the reader.

Those who died fuelled the fantasies of the killer and paid with their lives. By a long way, however, they are not the only victims.

The agony of a family:
Fiona Jones missing in France

Logic is not a cerebral, cold companion in life; on the contrary, it consoles and comforts, for it assures us that our routine expectations are indeed reasonable. It makes us feel safe, secure and optimistic to a degree we take far too much for granted. We depend upon logic to deliver life's normality in daily bundles and it is only when it fails us, when it falters and lets us down, that we despair of a world without rule or necessity.

It is the "contingent" world which Sartre described with horrific vividness and it is in such a world, viscous and hostile, that the family of Fiona Jones has lived for more than six weeks.

Fiona Jones went for a bicycle ride alone in France

on 14 August and vanished into nothingness, removed
from the face of the earth as surely as if she had been
snatched up by some demonic jackdaw. Both she and her
bicycle appear no longer to exist, because they are not there
for anybody to observe. Since 15 August Fiona's mother,
father, brother and husband have been trapped in this new
world where logic refuses to behave, and they are visibly
shaken by what they have been forced to contemplate. For
what happened to Fiona is impossible.

The facts are straightforward. Mark Jones, 26, whose
business is in sports equipment, had an appointment to discuss the design of a golf course at the Château de Bellinglise,
a large rather posh hotel in its own grounds about seven
miles from Compiègne in north-eastern France.

As he was about to celebrate the first anniversary of his
marriage to Fiona Cottrill, also 26, the couple decided
they would both go to France and stay on at the hotel
after Mark's business was over. They travelled from their
home, a pretty converted school house in the old village of
Kingsbury, Warwickshire, on Sunday 13 August, arriving
at Bellinglise late the same day.

Mark's appointment, which he would attend with his
partner Colin Snape, was for the next morning, after which
he and Fiona would have time to themselves.

On Monday morning Mark left Fiona in the hotel room,
where she indulged herself with breakfast in bed. She said
she would pass the time until he was free by hiring a bicycle
and going for a ride along the country road perhaps as
far as Compiègne. Bikes are readily available from the
hotel. She was given a metallic turquoise model by the
head receptionist and went happily up the drive towards
Route D142 at 11.30 a.m. She was wearing bright pink
shorts and a white top with short sleeves. It was a beautiful
day, warm, clear and windless.

Fiona cycled through the villages of Elincourt Ste
Marguerite and Marest-sur-Matz as far as the tiny hamlet

of Rimberlieu. We know this because she was seen by four motorists who either overtook her or passed in the opposite direction before 12.30.

Then there is a blank of two and a quarter hours when she was spotted by no one. The area is thickly wooded and below the woods there are fields high with corn. There are access roads to expensive private houses and paths into the woods, but no other road for traffic. Fiona may have taken a side turning to explore further.

I would have done the same, for the area is enchantingly pretty. There are no shops at Rimberlieu, just a few houses and a restaurant, La Bergerie, where the owner is cook, waiter and cleaner to the very occasional motorist who might stop. Apart from the passage of about four cars every minute, Rimberlieu is one of the most peaceful spots imaginable.

Fiona was seen again at 2.45 p.m., also at Rimberlieu, but facing the opposite direction. She was on her way back to the Château de Bellinglise; Mark had said to be home by 3.30 and she was in good time. She was drinking from a half-bottle of mineral water she had taken with her. Apart from that, she had only a 200-franc note (about £20) and the key-card to her hotel bedroom.

Mark Jones and Colin Snape had spent the morning in discussions with the two others, one of whom was an American golf architect. Their meeting at 8.30 a.m. had finished by 10.30 whereupon they all proceeded to examine the grounds. Then they had lunch at the hotel. Colin said, "Is Fiona joining us?" "No," said Mark, "she's gone out on a bike." Lunch was over by 2.30. One of the other businessmen was leaving for the airport and offered Colin a lift, but his flight was not until 7.30. "There's no hurry," said Mark. "Fiona will be back soon and we'll both take you." They lingered for the rest of the afternoon, had a cup of tea and waited.

When Fiona did not return by 5 p.m. Mark left a note

on her bed to say he had driven Colin to the airport and would be back after six, as indeed he was. The note had been moved to the sideboard which led Mark to believe his wife must be waiting for him somewhere in the hotel. She wasn't. The receptionist had not seen her since she left that morning. (Did a housekeeper move Mark's note? The bed had been made long before.)

Mark then drove the length of the road to Compiègne and back but found no sign of Fiona. He was alarmed and informed the police, though he still suspected she had got hopelessly lost and would probably turn up the next morning, dishevelled and distraught, having spent the night in a barn somewhere.

He looked forward to having to apologise to the gendarmerie for causing unnecessary trouble. At least Fiona spoke good French so she would not need to feel isolated and abandoned. As it later turned out, the motorist who saw her at 2.45 p.m. did not say she looked isolated or abandoned, nor even lost.

By Tuesday morning, alarm had turned to fear. Mark called his father in North Wales, Tony Jones. "Look, dad," he said, "I've got a problem. Fiona is missing. Should I tell Bruce and Pat (her parents) or wait until later? I don't want to upset them."

Tony Jones thought it was better to tell them straight away; he would do it as he lived just down the road from them. The two families had known each other for years. So Bruce Cottrill and his youngest son Simon went immediately to Manchester airport where they caught the first flight to Paris.

They were in Compiègne by Tuesday evening. They have been there ever since. Fiona's mother, Pat Cottrill, is there too, on her second visit. She once went home to Wales but could not bear the uncertainty at such a distance.

By this time Fiona was a "missing person". It was the audacity and determination of her frantic husband which turned the beneficent glare of international publicity upon the case.

He urged a colleague to inform Central TV, who in turn got in touch with their counterparts on French TV, and within 24 hours the Château de Bellinglise was besieged by over 150 reporters. Bruce Cotterill prepared a "Have you seen?" poster which he photocopied at the hotel and then distributed, with Simon, in every village on the route of Fiona's unfortunate journey and for miles around.

This was done by Wednesday. Meanwhile 50 policemen were joined by 40 volunteer firemen, and later 200 soldiers, to search the forests. Frogmen scoured the stagnant ponds which abound in the area and the underground tunnels dating from the First World War (the Armistice of 1918 was signed in the famous railway carriage which is still at Compiègne). Dogs were brought in and a helicopter flew low for a radius of 15 miles.

There was no sign whatever of either Fiona or her bicycle. On Wednesday evening, 16 August, the first, last and only clue was discovered by police. Fiona's hotel key-card lay in a field on the way out of Bellinglise. It was about 12 yards from the road.

There was nothing with it, no thread from clothing, no hair, nor any indication of a struggle. The clue was almost as silent as the mystery it should have dispelled.

Since then only the persistence of Fiona's family has made her presence felt. Captain Ster, the police chief in charge of the case, was obliged after eight days to follow French procedure and hand the matter over to a *juge d'instruction*, Madame Pagenelle, who may speak or not as she sees fit and is likely only to offer information if it is concrete and factual. She will not speculate and must not reveal the line of her enquiry however sympathetic she may be (and is) towards Mark Jones and the Cottrills.

So far there is nothing to relate. The police are now under her command but they are by their own admission *têtus* (stubborn) and will not rest until Fiona is found. To an especially crass English journalist who asked if they were looking for a body, Captain Ster said, "No, we are looking for Madame Jones."

Was that journalist merely voicing the thought in everybody's mind? What are the alternatives, in fact, to a tragic outcome? And who is Fiona Jones?

Bruce and Pat Cottrill started their family in Liverpool where their eldest child, Fiona, and their first son, Jonathan, ("Jonty", now 25) were born. Just before the birth of the third child, Simon (now 22), they moved to Old Colwyn in north Wales. It is a small community, friendly and supportive. Fiona, Jonty and Simon all went to the local school where another boy, Mark Jones, became a family friend.

By the time Mark was in the upper sixth, Fiona came into the lower sixth, and they began going to dances together. It was the beginning of a nine-year courtship. Fiona was pretty, with an open character and a ready smile. She was also academically bright, reading from the age of four, and by now a devoted admirer of Thomas Hardy.

She studied Italian and French at Leicester University and graduated with upper second-class honours. Meanwhile Mark decided to read for a civil engineering degree. He and Jonty both went up to Liverpool University where they graduated with honours.

Fiona's knack with languages enabled her to widen her reading still further. Dante became a great favourite, much to the amusement of Mark who found some of the stories "cracking" and far more risky than those in the Sunday papers.

Mark and Fiona married at Llanelian church in 1988. For Bruce, by now safety officer for Hotpoint in Llandudno, it was quite simply "the happiest day of our lives".

They set up home in Warwickshire where Fiona took a job as a primary school teacher. After work, when Mark returned from the office, they liked nothing better than to go out for a meal, particularly an Indian curry. At weekends Simon might come and stay. He was studying at Sheffield Polytechnic.

All perfectly ordinary and unremarkable. Until one day the French countryside swallowed Fiona Jones whole and refused to surrender her. Could she have met with an accident? Hospitals in the area were contacted. There was no accident. Could she have decamped, run off with someone, a new lover perhaps? Hardly. It would have been far easier to let Mark go to France and make her escape during his absence. And why would the elopers encumber themselves with a bicycle?

Fiona's photograph has been published in all corners of France; it is doubtful if she could have passed unnoticed for so long a time. And she left everything at the hotel, her passport, even her private building society account. An absconder does not walk into a new future so unprepared.

Despite all this, the flight theory is still the one most favoured by local barmen and gossips; in France everything boils down to illicit love. Has Fiona been kidnapped? This is the hope her family and husband cling to. Mark thinks it possible that kidnappers assumed she was from a rich family because she was staying at the Château de Bellinglise, and realised their mistake later.

Again, why bother to kidnap the bicycle as well? Mark experimented to see how long it would take to dismantle a bike and shove it into a car. Four minutes, during which time 20 cars could pass. A van, of course, could accommodate the bike easily, but then there would need to be more than one man to cope with Fiona *and* the bike.

Perhaps Mark Jones has organised the disappearance himself? He admits surprise that he was not told to surrender his passport and report to the police station every day (he does, but of his own accord). Colin Snape, who was with him the entire day of 14 August, has still not been questioned by anyone. The idea is obviously too fanciful to merit investigation and has rightly been dismissed by the police.

Another possibility is that Fiona wandered back into the forest for an unknown reason and got into difficulties, in this case, the army, the police, the firemen, the dogs, the frogmen and the helicopter have all passed her by.

The harshest scenario holds that Fiona has been the victim of a crime, that she has been taken for loathsome purposes and that she will only be released, if at all, when the criminal or criminals have been satisfied.

Route D142 is not a road to travel if you are looking for a potential victim. Far better to try Paris or the Côte d'Azure. If Fiona fell into the clutches of ruthless men, then they were travelling on the least likely road and encountered their prey entirely by accident. The snatch would have been impulsive. Did they then throw the key-card into the field? No, it weighs little and would not travel 12 yards. Fiona dropped it in the field.

The question again arises, why bother to steal the bicycle as well? What else? Amnesia? She would have turned up by now. Imprisonment by an innocent madman who wants company, like Clegg in John Fowles's *The Collector*? This is an attractive idea, for at least Fiona would be unlikely to come to any harm. On the other hand the collector might keep her for months.

Meanwhile Fiona Jones's family stay on in Compiègne, assaulted by these corrosive thoughts, and more, every day. They have a flat which has been given to them indefinitely by a well-wisher.

They rarely eat out, but are seen walking in the town, where everyone recognises them and keeps a respectful distance. Pat Cottrill is the kind of naturally elegant woman one would want to meet and talk with, but circumstances forbid. Bruce Cottrill reveals the weight of worry in his face.

They are never apart. They would each cry, with Juliet,

Is there no pity sitting in the clouds
That sees into the bottom of my grief?

Mark is white-faced and weary. He goes into the
gendarmerie every day simply to establish that he will not
cease until something is discovered. "I must do everything
possible to help my wife," he says. "They know I am going
to turn up every day. They can't forget about the case."

Talking with this tall, good-looking man, one makes a
conscious effort to speak of Fiona in the present tense, but
in the end it is not entirely honest to smother thoughts in
this way.

After a couple of hours, Mark grabs the thorn. "We have
thought about it in circles," he says. "You are an outsider.
Tell me what you think. What are the chances that my wife
is still alive?" I reply that I give her more than a 50 per
cent chance, because I pin hopes on the harmless lonely
madman who wants to look at her.

Simon Cottrill spends much of the day playing computer
chess. He will soon have to make a hard decision. He is due
to begin a course at Leeds University and will have to leave
Compiègne.

Simon is scrupulously honest with his thoughts. I suggest
we go for a drink and I am careful, for once, not to talk
about Fiona but to be light and discursive. "It is more false
to talk about something else," he says, "and pretend that
Fiona is not on our minds. Even to think about something
else is a kind of disloyalty, a failure of love." So we talk
about Fiona. When she turns up, I will want to wean her
off Hardy and introduce her to Anthony Trollope. That,
I hope, will be my small share of the celebration.

Evening Standard, 25 September 1989.

The pain of a spared victim: Carl Stottor two years after the Nilsen trial

The most dramatic moment in the trial of Dennis Nilsen at the Old Bailey just over two years ago came when a young man called Carl Stottor stood nervously in the witness-box, and in a barely audible voice described how the defendant had first strangled him, then drowned him in the bath, to within seconds of death, ignoring his pitiful pleas for mercy.

What made the story especially bizarre was that Nilsen, who had confessed to killing 15 men in this manner, carried Stottor's apparently lifeless body into the bedroom and dumped it. Only Nilsen's pet dog's attention in licking the corpse some minutes later revealed the dim flickers of life, whereupon Nilsen, instead of despatching him, spent the next 24 hours reviving him with extra blankets, heating, and body warmth.

He then escorted him to the tube station, with the glib explanation that Stottor had caught his neck in the zipper of the sleeping-bag.

The mystery which hung over the courtroom, and with which psychiatrists would hopelessly grapple, was why the defendant should change character so drastically. For no one was the mystery more serious than for Stottor himself.

"Is Nilsen my murderer or my saviour?" he now asks. "I don't know how I should feel about him. There have been times when I wish he had left me for dead."

In a quite dreadful way, Carl Stottor is still Nilsen's victim.

Little time is spent considering the psychological and emotional damage endured by those few people who survive a vicious attempt to kill them. They are thought lucky to be alive. In fact, as Stottor's subsequent history shows, their ethical understanding can be shattered, their moral values besieged, their human relationships poisoned. Quite apart from his obvious fear of going anywhere alone or speaking to any stranger, Carl Stottor feels that his most cherished intimacy, with his family, has been destroyed.

During the attack, he had lapsed into unconsciousness so frequently that his recollection was impaired. "I can remember, but I can't see the pictures. I have no pictures." Only very gradually over the coming weeks did portions of the nightmare return, and when he first reflected that indeed someone may have tried to kill him, he told his mother, who ridiculed the suggestion and told him that the sensation of drowning was a childhood memory.

She now feels guilt for having made her son doubt, and he still feels betrayed by her. The rift has widened since the trial, and they rarely see each other.

His grandmother, with whom he had been very close since childhood, he never visits at all, for she is reminded of the ghastliness of what happened every time she sees him, and he must spare her the repeated distress. Then there was his little sister, to whom he had to explain that his head had not been boiled in a pot.

"With all the members of my family, there is now a barrier," says Stottor. "I always loved my mother, but there's no contact between us now. It's as if I'm dead. I sometimes feel that myself. Everything I do, see, touch, it's not me that's touching it. Something in me has gone."

It was not until months after the attack, when the police tracked him down from sparse information given by Nilsen – he was performing sporadically on pub stages as a drag artist – that he knew for certain his morbid imaginings were based on fact. The biggest surprise was that his attacker had been Nilsen, a man whom he remembered as kind and helpful. (He had thought his attacker must have been a man he knew in Blackpool.) He had been drawn to Nilsen, and had wished he could be lucky enough to find someone as decent as that to live with. Had he not lost the address, he would almost certainly have gone back to visit Nilsen again.

That his trust should have been so misplaced has made Stottor uncertain of everything. For about six months after the trial, he was in the grip of severe depression. He drank all day, rarely ate, and then nearly always vomited, lost the will to get out of bed or go anywhere. Depression was followed by fear, and fear by continual nightmares. One of the nastiest facts he had to absorb was that one of those murdered, John Howletts, was from the same town, High Wycombe; Howletts's father had once worked with Stottor's mother. As John Howletts met his death in March 1982, and Carl Stottor's appalling 48 hours in Nilsen's flat took place in April, Howletts's slumped body was in the cupboard in the next room throughout the ordeal. Yet in the nightmares, Stottor hears himself uttering terms of endearment to Nilsen as well as fear.

Not surprisingly, he began to fear for his sanity. Two hospitals turned him away. "I begged them to lock me up, but they just wouldn't listen." He still wonders how his infected imagination will behave in years to come. "You cannot just take something out of your head and throw it away."

He thought of hypnotherapy but he was advised that, having narrowly survived the first time, if he relived the attempted murder he may not survive again.

In desperation, Carl Stottor next went to social workers in Blackfriars and lived for nearly a year in a house of homeless young people where discussion and group therapy were encouraged. He is now back in lodgings in High Wycombe and has an occasional evening job. His hair went grey, so he dyed it, and he has not yet conquered the tension, which manifests itself by inappropriate laughter at the end of every sentence. He is 25 years old.

What was he like before he encountered Nilsen? It was by no means an idyllic, carefree childhood: a hated father, parents divorced when he was 13, a few months in a children's home before living with his grandmother.

But it was productive. He worked in a linen shop, joined the London Festival Ballet as an extra, danced with Blackpool's local group The Silhouettes, painted pictures, made toys, wrote poems. He was active.

He had ambition, too, and hoped to stay in show business. "Perhaps I was only chasing dreams, but he has taken them away. I'll never be anything now." He can accept the change, but his mother says she does not know him any more.

Worst of all is his inability to escape the past. "At least if I keep it to myself I am not hurting anyone else. But I can't stop talking about it either. I'm possessive about it. It's *mine*, something that gives me feelings."

Stottor says he cannot feel much genuinely about anything else. He sometimes gets up in the middle of the night and starts scribbling. He is usually writing something which revolves around emotions he used to have, "inventing emotions for myself, since I can't feel anything." At other times he writes about the attack on his life.

A psychoanalyst might unravel the knotted ball of motives, illusions and distortions which churn in the head of this young man who clings to a frightful memory in spite of himself. He has even thought he might like to visit Nilsen in prison, as a kind of cathartic exercise, and with this in mind is in correspondence with him.

Though it is difficult for him to admit, I suspect part of his problem is a *frisson* at having been so intimate with evil and a desire to enjoy it again and again. So powerful is the evil force that it can bewitch by association, and when Stottor says he can forgive his murderer, it is a seductive, deceptive way of getting closer to him. "I know I'm a statistic," he says, "victim of crime and violence. I will always be Nilsen's victim. In a horrible way we've been thrown together."

Nilsen, too, has reflected upon having a victim who is

still alive. "I feel disturbed with nausea when I am reminded
of the suffering which I have caused to Carl Stottor," he
wrote recently. "I feel responsible and sorry for his plight
. . . Whatever I was trying to "kill", it was *not* him."

The Observer, 18 May 1986.

The search for bodies in a back garden

Local children called it the House on the Hill. Tall, square,
imposing and mysterious, it dominated the road at Clapton
Common, east London, in both directions. It had once been
a school for the deaf, and when that closed, the big building
remained empty for a number of years. A long dirt track
at the side led to a huge back garden, overgrown and
virtually impassable through years of neglect. Beyond that
lay the beautiful wilderness of Springfield Park, common
land often used for purposes better pursued in private.

The children did not dare venture down the path to
that dense garden, which was just as well, for police now
believe that the garden served as a makeshift grave for an
adolescent boy killed in the course of a sexual act. Had the
soil been dug over a year or more ago, it may well have
yielded its gruesome secret, but in the meantime the big,
square building has become a synagogue, an addition has
been built at the back, and the rest of the garden has been
flattened into a car park. To achieve this, bulldozers had
to remove the top two feet of earth, and the operators of
bulldozers do not generally see what they are digging up.
Murder victims are not usually buried very deep, so the
likelihood is that the remains of this boy have disappeared
forever, taking with them the clue to his fate.

There is something especially fearful about the disposal of a dead body. In various discussions with the serial murderer Dennis Nilsen seven years ago, I made plain my horror at the dismemberment of a once-living person, a response which he found bewildering. The unforgivable thing, he said, was to squeeze the life out of a man, but a corpse could not be hurt, and to protest indignation at an act which was merely efficient was morally questionable. That may be logical, but it is abnormal. Respect for the dead ascends beyond the evolution of a moral sense to something fundamental, and its absence distinguishes a murderer from the rest of us more bluntly than the killing itself. That is why digging beneath a car park for what is left of an unmourned child offends the very soul.

For the past two weeks, the police have been churning up a corner of the car park and have found crushed bone fragments. Many of these have been declared to be of non-human origin; it remains to be determined whether some are human remains.

But even if the bones are not human, the investigation will continue. Dogs have already confirmed the presence of human remains, whose scent endures for up to ten years, and though the press has only just been alerted to what is going on, the enquiry has continued in the utmost secrecy for 12 months. A number of charges have already been brought and many more are expected, including possibly well over ten indictments for murder. Other related charges involving buggery and homosexual offences against minors could involve hundreds of people.

For Detective Chief Superintendent Roger Stoodley already knows that there are several other sites where bodies have been interred. He suspects there may be 12 bodies, but does not discount the possibility of more. Stoodley's information is solid and he is confident that a lot of people are feeling apprehensive. The enquiry, which he hopes to conclude within the next few months, promises to uncover a sordid and widespread criminal conspiracy.

Mr Stoodley will not reveal the name of his informant. Nor will he confirm whether he is serving time, whether he is part of the conspiracy, whether he has pointed fingers at suspects. It is better that everyone should be kept guessing, and the tension has already flushed out a number of people prepared to talk. The enquiry has been kept so confidential that only three other officers are entirely aware of Mr Stoodley's careful strategy. The tentacles of his search have spread way beyond the East End of London to other parts of the country and abroad, and most recently have brought him to question an inmate at Albany Prison. What they discussed remains a secret.

A sensitive and sensible man, Mr Stoodley makes plain his abhorrence of sexual exploitation, while understanding how easily wickedness might evolve out of something intrinsically decent. Parents who abuse their children, he points out, often care for them lovingly and provide an otherwise happy and stable home life. One might also say that the instinct of an older man to befriend a youngster is common enough, and not always harmful. But when groups of men gang up to use a boy as an object in an orgy of selfishness, the result is an ugly perversion of the gentleness which ought to lie at the heart of human relationships, and which has nothing whatever to do with friendship. The dig at Clapton Common, and others to come, exposes the evil which is but one step beyond sexual licence.

It is by no means easy for police officers to be vigilant of their own emotions when dealing with an investigation as unpleasant as this. Detective Chief Inspector Peter Jay, who arrested Dennis Nilsen in 1983, confessed to feeling nauseated when the various pieces of Nilsen's last victim were assembled on the mortuary floor. Officers are not always inured to suffering. They have imaginations as well as experience, and it may be that Peter Topping, who resurrected the search for victims of the Moors Murderers

Ian Brady and Myra Hindley 20 years after the event, was moved by pity for the unrelieved plight of the parents of those children still unaccounted for.

There are no clues to the identities of the victims in the present enquiry. Thousands of adolescent boys go missing, and a good proportion of them never return home. One who personified the vulnerability of such boys was 14-year-old Jason Swift, with whose violent death – in a Hackney council flat not far from Clapton Common – this enquiry began. Consider what happened to him. He was befriended by men, flattered and made a fuss of. He was frequently buggered – probably with consent, for an odd fiver. One night he found himself with four men, Sidney Cooke, Robert Oliver, Stephen Barrell and Leslie Bailey. They gave him pills to dull his responses. One sodomised him while another held his throat and, in an excess of lust, blocked his windpipe. His body was bathed and left in the flat overnight, then dumped beneath bracken some miles away. At the ensuing trial, some jurors wept openly; all four men are now serving prison sentences for his manslaughter. If the current enquiry succeeds, some good, though not to Jason Swift, will have come from his death.

The Independent on Sunday, 10 June 1990.

The murder of Simon Dale

Scarcely anyone now remembers the name of Simon Dale, but there are many who will recall the exotic name of his former wife, Baroness de Stempel, charged with and acquitted of his murder last year, thus demonstrating yet again that the accused is always more fascinating to the

public than the victim. Earlier this year she pleaded guilty
to five counts of theft and two of forgery, after having
systematically stripped her aged and ailing aunt, Lady
Illingworth, of everything she owned. Lady Illingworth is
now dead too, anonymously dumped at a crematorium.
But what of Simon Dale, father of her five children? Found
lying in blood on the blue and white tiled kitchen floor
of his home between Hopton Castle and Leintwardine in
Shropshire on 13 September 1987, the loss of his life was
a mere prelude to the theft of his character and reputation
in court, apparently for ever.

He must have fought hard to evade his assailant, as blood
was found beyond the kitchen, and he was a strong man,
6ft 3in tall and very fit for his 68 years. But he would
not have been able to know where the next blow was
coming from, as he raised his arms wildly for protection,
for he was almost totally blind.

At Susan de Stempel's trial, Dale was depicted as a dotty
recluse who for 14 years had refused to dislodge himself
from her property, who had beaten her and terrified their
children, who had on occasion worn high-heel shoes and
lipstick, and who was condemned from the witness-box as
a man who "needed sex to satisfy himself". There was no
one to stand up and defend Mr Dale – not one of his friends
and neighbours was called to give evidence. Thus, while the
case against Susan de Stempel was thrown out by a jury,
the case against Simon Dale rests unchallenged. It is about
time this was put right, if only on the grounds that justice
for the dead might be as desirable as acquittal for the living.

Simon Dale was essentially an acquiescent man, not fond
of dispute and by no means dogmatic or harsh in opinion or
manner. He was known locally as "the gentle giant" since
he was never seen to lose his temper, despite the affliction of
creeping blindness and the irritations attendant upon living
alone in the dark. He smiled, he chuckled, he welcomed,
but he did not complain. As Susan Sole, who lives in

Bodenham, Herefordshire said, "he was such a gentle person to meet such a violent end". Far from being a recluse, he was gregarious to a degree, and enjoyed the company of a regular and loyal group of friends. His culinary invention was naturally limited to what he could feel. He made the best baked potatoes in their jackets in the county, and there was a toad-in-the-hole burning in the oven when his body was found. When friends dropped in they would each bring a course and a spontaneous dinner party would ensue, Simon making dry, witty remarks in a resonant voice which filled the empty air in front of his eyes with sparkle.

He made his own marmalade every year, though a new recipe he once attempted did stump him. Having telephoned for help, "come quick, my marmalade's gone wrong", it transpired he had cut up the oranges and soaked them overnight, with newspaper covering the top of the pan, then stirred the newspaper in with the ingredients in the morning. Such a cosy tale hardly fits the characteristics of a monster.

The house in which he lived and died was Heath House, a large seventeenth-century redbrick mansion with one of the finest oak staircases in the country, rising either side of the hall, meeting and separating through connecting galleries to the top of the house. It probably came from Hopton Castle, sacked in the Civil War.

This area of south-west Shropshire is peaceful and remote, almost arrested in time. The sheep were there before the Civil War, the roads follow medieval tracks, there are no pylons and no neon signs. Hamlets rather than villages are scattered over a large area, nestling behind hills, wooded in meandering valleys, and the people who live in them know each other's business because human contact, however distant, becomes more than ever important in a land passed over by the frantic activities of the twentieth century.

Dale was an architect by profession, attached to a firm

in Birmingham. At the age of 33 he had begun to lose his sight through an hereditary misfortune which no medicine can alleviate or arrest, and which one of his sons has been told will befall him also in time. In 1957 he married Susan Wilberforce, daughter of a prominent Yorkshire family whose ancestry went back to the Middle Ages (they took their name from a village near York called Wild Boar Foss), and whose most illustrious member had been William Wilberforce, the MP who is revered for having abolished slavery. It was said that Simon felt sorry for her, since she was already isolated from her family. Two years later they bought Heath House for £2,000, saving an architectural jewel from imminent demolition, and taking on a burden which would try their marriage and ultimately fuel the gnawing antagonism that replaced it.

The Dales had five children in seven years: William; Ilgerius Sebastian (Illgerus of Eagleton had been a Wilberforce forebear at the time of Edward I); Xenophon Marcus; Simon Quintin; and at last a girl – Georgina Sophia. Then Susan Dale left Heath House, taking most of the children with her, and moved to the village of Docklow some 27 miles away, although Sebastian was brought up mostly by his father. In 1973 they were divorced. Solicitors suggested they should each reveal their income and its source so that a just settlement could be reached, but Susan refused. Hence Simon stayed on in the marital home which had been bought in Susan's name. Years later, he told his farming friend Ken Davison, "I made a terrible mistake in not having the house in our joint names." For 12 years, however, Susan did not disturb his peace. The version given in court that she had been trying to get rid of him for 14 years was not accurate.

As Simon's sight deteriorated, he was obliged to abandon his only source of earned income as an architect, after which he developed a growing obsession with the house and its history. Bravely walking alone to the station, with tunnel vision obscuring everything but a pinpoint, he took the train to Shrewsbury to research the records of the Roman provinces; he had a theory that the Romans employed Turks and that an Armenian religious site existed somewhere under the cellars of Heath House. He would ask a friend to hold two iron rods in front of her, and triumphantly point to their gradually coming together, which proved the presence of an Armenian lavatory. Marie-Louise Osborne, who held the rods, said, "Do shut up, Simon, they're meeting because they're so heavy I can't carry them." He wasn't solemn about his theories and was often happily teased about them, but he did laboriously write them up in language so erudite and learned (and so badly typed) that none of the country folk felt up to understanding such intellectual moonshine. Nevertheless they admired his persistence. He would dig a hole in the drive, and ask neighbours to look into it – their function to describe, his to interpret.

Another of his studies was into the working of the optic nerve, advancing a theory that the day would come when the human eye could have images imprinted by human agency. This led him towards a treatise on the brain, which grew to a whole paper, never published.

Simon Dale was wonderfully easy about his blindness, so that his visitors would never feel they had to dissemble or avoid the subject. He would find one object on his plate ("tell me where the peas are, at 11 o'clock?") and divine the position of the rest accordingly. When mowing the lawn, he placed an empty yoghurt carton on the ground, its whiteness acting as a guide, and then felt his way among the trees. He even went so far as to take tea on a sunny afternoon in the garden, with cucumber sandwiches cut like crazy paving. "Do you fancy a crumpet tea?" he would call, then walk the three miles to the village to buy the crumpets. Friends darned his pullover for him so often that there was hardly anything left of the original garment.

Mrs Dale, who had reverted to the name Wilberforce and persuaded her children, all Dales, to do the same, married *en secondes noces* Baron Michael-Victor-Jossif Walter von Stempel (known as Baron de Stempel), a descendant of an ancient Westphalian family ennobled by the Holy Roman Empire in 1369, and himself an erstwhile officer in the Royal Irish Fusiliers and the Royal Ulster Rifles. They had known each other for a number of years.

De Stempel was excitable, blunt, and apparently scared stiff of his wife. At the committal proceedings preceding her arraignment for murder, he blurted out that she had tried to have him committed to a lunatic asylum, and he could scarcely be contained by the bemused magistrate. The marriage lasted less than a year, but in the course of it Baroness de Stempel initiated a plot to defraud her aunt and fleece her before it was too late, for which offences she was recently convicted. She also turned her attentions to her former husband, Simon Dale, and began to show up unexpectedly at Heath House.

Susan de Stempel sought opportunities for confrontation, but the object of rousing Simon Dale to anger always eluded her, a failure which naturally infuriated her even more. The stories he told of her attempts to, shall we say, affect his mood, sound like the grim humour of Punch and Judy or a Grand Guignol farce. She placed heavy logs outside the front door; she threw hot coals at him; she hid his stick. Simon was stubbornly philosophical about the whole thing, relating these events with a relaxed, indifferent air. "By the way," he would say, "the latest on the domestic front is that she kicked me in the balls yesterday."

She also took to pouncing upon his visitors. Veronica Bowater, a local historian and friend, turned up at Heath House one day with a meal she had prepared, to be welcomed by Susan de Stempel advancing upon her with a blow-torch. In her confusion, she said, "Mrs Wilberforce, I presume," a mistake which drew the imperious response,

"I am the Baroness de Stempel." For two years Ken Davison had grazed 12 of his sheep in the field at the front of Heath House, until he arrived with them in the van one day to be accosted by the Baroness, who had heard the bleating. "What have you got in there?" she said. "I'm going to put my sheep here to graze." "Oh no, you're not," she flared. "Everything here belongs to *me*; house, garden, furniture, every bloody thing." Davison left with his sheep.

The third son, Marcus, spent a couple of nights a week at Heath House and Simon's friends colluded to find him work amongst themselves as a jobbing gardener. He also knew a great deal about bee-keeping. As part of the plan, Marcus spent a summer in Germany, with his bicycle, and worked as a trainee landscape gardener. His host, a German barrister called Wolfgang Reidar, visited England some months later with his wife Margarethe and was invited by Simon to drinks at Heath House, where they hoped to see Marcus again. While Marcus hid behind the bushes in the garden, his mother flew at the Reidar's car, blow-torch to the fore, arms waving frantically and face as black as thunder. She kicked the car furiously. The German, still at the driving-wheel, was astonished to say the least. "Look at her eyes," he said. "She's quite mad." The Baroness always seemed to know when guests would be arriving, as she was on the spot at the crucial moment, and it was suggested that she had her ex-husband's telephone tapped so she would know when anyone was coming. To one startled visitor she said, "What are you doing beside my car? I suppose you're preparing to damage it," Another received the warning, "I wouldn't go in that house if I were you. Sophia went in last week and got bitten with fleas." Marcus was once discovered kneeling on the floor behind the kitchen door, apparently spying on the visitors, until he was politely told not to be so silly and to come on in.

As this relentless persecution continued, with ornaments gradually disappearing from a house whose occupant was blind and was powerless to intercede, the "gentle giant" began to voice some alarm, expressed in a jocular, mock-serious manner. "She'll have me one day," he once said. Someone might be heard roaming around the house while Simon Dale was lunching with friends. On one occasion Susan de Stempel was seen peering through the dining-room window at her ex-husband's guests.

In addition, there was pressure upon the children to take sides in an increasingly acrimonious squabble. Marcus, who would be said in court to walk in fear of his father, showed no such signs in reality, even inviting people from London to stay at the house, something a frightened individual would be unlikely to attempt. His mother, on the other hand, did sometimes give cause for anxiety, according to local wisdom. The epithets which began to circulate concerning her were far from complimentary. She was termed "evil" and "unscrupulous" by people who had had the chance to contemplate her behaviour for a protracted period.

The last son to discard the surname Dale was Sebastian, who worked for a while at the Conservative Central Office. Simon was observed to be upset the first time he heard his son referred to as "Wilberforce", and to ask if it were really true that he had changed his name. The impression was that the maternal influence had been strong. It was "sickening", said an inhabitant of Leintwardine, "to see Sebastian trying to ingratiate himself with his own mother." Sebastian wisely refused to take sides, but his continuing desire to see his father did not place him in good favour with his mother.

There followed the horrific murder of September 1987, and the subsequent trial two years later. Baroness de Stempel, Marcus Wilberforce and Sophia Wilberforce were arrested and charged with the murder of Simon Dale. The charges against Marcus and Sophia were dropped three weeks later, but that against the Baroness was proceeded with, despite there being no forensic evidence to link her with the death of her ex-husband. Of circumstantial evidence there was a plethora, including some of the foregoing information which was given to the police in statements. Simon had been killed by blows from a heavy object, which could have been a jemmy or a crow-bar. His ex-wife had acquired a new one, which she made no attempt to disguise or conceal, and which she said was for clearing the brambles. (No one in court pointed out that jemmies are singularly ineffective in clearing brambles!) The final blow to the Adam's apple could have been caused by a poker similar to one found at her cottage in Docklow, but there was no blood on it, or in her cottage.

In the dock, the Baroness conducted herself with extra-ordinary coolness, an almost icy control, and fastidious superiority. Small and mouse-like, with a tiny voice, what she lacked in stature she made up for in cheek. In answer to one question, she replied, "Bollocks" in that lyrical, sing-song, devil-may-care intonation which is habitually adopted by children who have been caught out and don't give a damn. At the later hearing in Birmingham, as charges of theft and forgery were read out, she again replied "guilty" in a manner which suggested she was bored with the whole business, her hands thrust down in the pockets of her donkey-jacket, looking at her watch, staring at the ceiling, with the suggestion of a swinging motion as she changed feet to relieve the tedium.

Susan de Stempel was acquitted of the murder of Simon Dale, and her innocence means that his murderer is still at large. There is no clue as to who it might be, except that a mysterious hitch-hiker, never traced, was seen in the vicinity of Heath House that Saturday evening. But hitch-hikers do not normally kill blind men in their own homes, if only because it is not an efficient way of getting a lift. Which leaves one with a blank, empty, featureless and unsatisfactory conclusion – that a brave, stoical, re-silient, donnish and charming gentleman was murdered

by a person or persons unknown for absolutely no reason
that anyone can imagine.

His reputation, however, also murdered in court, is
capable of being rescued. "There was nothing nasty about
this man," said Susan Sole. "He was a darling. To have him
spoken of like this in court was horrible." Lady Ransome,
widow of Sir Gordon Ransome, who lives in Presteigne,
told me that the people from this quiet, somnolent corner
of Shropshire near the Welsh borders desperately want it
known that Simon was traduced and blackened without
redress. They feel that a miscarriage of justice lay in the
fact that lies were told about the victim of a brutal murder,
and that no one saw fit to question them because the
character of a dead man, whose achievements were private
and unproclaimed, does not in the end matter very much.
"He gave such richness to the tapestry of life in this area,"
said Veronica Bowater. "We miss him very much."

Everyone in the area is now apprehensive about the
future of Heath House, the more so in view of its unhappy
past. For Dale's death was not the only suspicious fatality
to occur there. Around 1970, Arthur Prime, the husband
of a woman patient who died, held her doctor responsible.
Bent upon vengeance, Prime persuaded the medic into his
own car, drove him into the grounds of Heath House and
shot him dead with a 12-bore. At his trial he was declared
insane and shut away for a number of years. He is in
the *Guinness Book of Records* for the largest number of
O levels ever achieved – over 30.

Friends plan to hold a memorial service for Simon Dale
at the ancient church which stands in the middle of a
field at Hopton Castle, within sight of the ruins of the
castle itself. It was there, you will recall, that the oak
staircase of Heath House originated.

                              Harpers & Queen, May 1990.

Living with murder

In her book *For the Love of Lesley*, reissued next week in a revised edition, Ann West, the mother of pitiful Moors victim Lesley Ann Downey, speaks of "the unique agony of losing a child or loved one to a murderer". Those simple, stark words reveal a truth which, mercifully, few of us are ever called upon to face. Grief is common enough and acceptable. It may even yield a kind of solace, as the performance of grieving confirms the bonds of love which unite the survivor and the departed. But grief cannot be pure if it is brutally forced upon one by the act of a stranger who insultingly intrudes himself into those ties of blood and affection. It may become contaminated by guilt, anger, hatred and spiritual depression. Mrs West's "life sentence of grief", as she puts it, may well be an illustration of this. Nearly 30 years after her daughter's disappearance, her pain is unrelieved. She is, in a way, possessed by it.

Such an observation must not in any sense be considered a rebuke. For if losing somebody to a murderer is unique, Mrs West's dreadful experience stands out within that uniqueness as utterly without comparison. Not only did little Lesley Ann, aged ten, fall victim to the foul fantasies of Brady and Hindley, but her torture and humiliation were recorded by them on tape. Anyone who heard or read of those tapes wept with her, and indeed the country has never recovered from the horror of them. Yet it is permissible to wonder whether other ways of dealing with the pain, and eventually emerging from it, might be just as valid.

Gordon Wilson, whose daughter Marie was murdered by the IRA in the Enniskillen bombing of 1987, told me a few weeks ago, "there is no list of rules for dealing with sudden bereavement". His own response was immediate and justly famous. He prayed for the souls of Marie's

killers, a gesture which elicited praise from the Queen in
her Christmas message as well as humility in the population
as a whole. Of course, the two incidents are not obviously
analogous. For one thing, there is usually a suffocating
feeling of self-chastisement which precedes any coming-
to-terms with what has happened. Lesley Ann Downey's
14-year-old brother Terry languished for years in the belief
that her death was his fault for not having been with her at
the time. How much worse must it be, then, for a mother.

Diana Lamplugh, whose daughter Suzy disappeared
without trace following an appointment with "Mr Kipper",
concedes that some of her initial grief consisted in "remorse
and guilt, which I know is completely ridiculous, and I tried
to recognise it." Ridiculous or not, it is virtually automatic
and actually necessary. Mrs Lamplugh, an impressive and
sensible lady, lost her temper with me only once. I was
telling her how I had accompanied the parents of Fiona
Jones (at their invitation) at the trial in France of Fiona's
killer Frédéric Blancke and sat with them in court trans-
lating proceedings on a pad which I passed along for
Mrs Cottrill, the mother, to read. There were moments
when I stayed my pen, in a foolish attempt to protect her
from the most searing details. "How *dare* you?" cried Mrs
Lamplugh. "She has an absolute *right* to know, to suffer.
Fiona was part of her body. A mother has a positive need
to relieve her child's pain, it is part of her function in
motherhood to relieve it. She has got to hear that pain and
know in what it consisted." It was then that I understood
why the self-flagellation (why wasn't I *there*?) should be
inevitable and in a sense placatory. Once again, it reasserts
the bond. Pat Cottrill agreed. She did not want to be
protected.

"A mother's grief is quite different from a father's,"
concedes Gordon Wilson, who experienced none of that
guilt of absence, having held Marie's hand as they lay
together beneath the rubble.

Mrs Lamplugh is equally adamant, however, that bereaved persons must move on from there, otherwise
suffering can be cherished too long and self-chiding
become a new way of life. They are frequently prevented
from taking this step by the attentions of journalists. "It
distresses me that some people's tragedies are fed on and
prolonged by those around them," she says, "perhaps to
secure some vicarious excitement. This is very detrimental.
People who have been bereaved in this brutal way need
helpful management to move on, and yet society seems
at times not to want them to. We, the parents of murder
victims, seem disrespectful if we do move on, as if we're
spoiling their story. It's appalling. I know the parents of
children who died on the moors. They have been so fed
upon by people and journalists, who consider it *their* cause,
that they have been enclosed in a web and drained dry. They
appear to have nothing left but their tragedy."

This is perhaps what Mrs West tacitly admits when she
writes, "Lesley and what happened to her has given me
something to live for." She has allowed her tragedy to be
kidnapped by the press.

Colin Parry, father of 12-year-old Tim, who was blasted
away by the Warrington bomb earlier this year, already
recognises the need to go forward, and will resist the attentions of those who would suck him and his wife Wendy
into a spurious "club" of historic victims. "We must maintain our friendships as well as make new ones," he says.
"No way could we only have people in our lives who
are similarly bereaved parents."

There are many occasions, in assembling this article, that
I have myself felt intrusive and apologetic, not because I
might appear to look for a display of emotion, but because
I should acknowledge the intimate privacy of grief and,
perhaps, not accept the commission to write about it at
all. The families of murder victims do not see it like this
at all. In the short term, they are grateful for press attention

because it affords them an opportunity to talk. Colin Parry welcomed the chance to celebrate his son Tim in conversations with journalists. I remember an occasion at the trial of Jeffrey Dahmer in Milwaukee when, after we had listened to disgusting evidence relating to the death of Eddie Smith, Eddie's sister Theresa came and sat next to me to show me snapshots she carried with her of Eddie playing a guitar, Eddie laughing, Eddie being alive. It was poignant and it was good, a quiet but eloquent denial of evil.

Similarly in Beauvais and Compiègne, the Cottrills were not at all reluctant, while I approached the subject obliquely and gingerly, to talk about Fiona. Mrs Lamplugh is willing to speak for subtly different reasons. "I wouldn't talk to you just to pick over it all again," she told me. "I do it because I hope it might enable others, else I wouldn't have agreed to see you at all."

It is when press attention becomes predatory that the danger arises of victims' families being submerged by the possessiveness which Mrs Lamplugh abhors. In an impassioned passage in her book, Mrs West tells us what she would like to respond to that crass and puerile question "How do you feel?", a question which she says "rapes you of your deepest inner sorrow". "I feel a deep longing to be dead," she writes. "I feel I want to kill those who are responsible for that body on a cold slab. I feel I want to take your cameras and your microphones and . . ." If only somebody would say that, perhaps editors would be chastened into educating their cub reporters in elementary sensitivity.

The first great swell of true therapy for the family comes with the ritual lamentation of a public funeral. Mrs West has never forgotten the crowds who turned out to bid farewell to Lesley Ann Downey, and the parents of Tim Parry are still visibly overwhelmed when they recall what Warrington did. "The funeral cortège passed in front of Tim's school," says his mother Wendy. "I've never seen so many children in tears. The whole town came to a standstill, every door opened, every housewife stood on the doorstep, every car stopped, every lorry-driver got out of his cab and stood. The procession behind Tim's coffin was four miles long. Police saluted the cortège as we went by. It was very moving." Colin takes up the story. "It makes you realise you are not alone. All those people bonded with us, even if it was for but a short time. You realise how good people are, on the whole."

This realisation must be essential to the renewal of self, and to keep ruinous bitterness at bay. It balances and should ideally neutralise the evil which has suddenly infected an ordinary life. Mr Parry is not a religious man, but he is eager to pay tribute to the help he received from religious men. "A Roman Catholic priest turned up at the hospital the day before Tim died. I didn't particularly want him around, but I let him in because I wouldn't cause offence. He said a very moving prayer by Tim's side, and then did something very simple, something nobody else had done up till then. He said, will you tell me about Tim? It was just what I needed. I talked and talked. He didn't interrupt, and I could tell he was really listening. That did me a power of good."

The televised funeral was led by the local vicar. "He was a bag of nerves. I liked that frailty in him. In their different ways, the priest and the vicar showed me their humanity." Mrs West pays similar tribute to the love offered by men of the church.

Not surprisingly, Mr Parry finds that the spiritual element is far sharper in his life than it ever was before the tragedy. Of the priest, who is sure that God gave him Tim as a helper, he says, "I now need his beliefs. I have a deep longing to see Tim again. I hope for some proof that the spirit continues. I can't go on longing for the next 30 years, to feel his presence and to be with him, without some result."

The earthly reflection of spiritual continuance is to keep Tim's name alive, and in this Mr Parry echoes the need of

many parents in his position whose bereavement has been
dramatic. Certainly, we all remember our loved ones in
anecdote and fond reminiscence, but the victim of a murder
should somehow be recalled more monumentally. The best
example is Mrs Lamplugh who, denied the dignity of a
funeral (her daughter has never been found), established
the Suzy Lamplugh Trust both to educate people in how
to protect themselves in the streets and to help the families
of murder victims to reconstruct their optimism and confidence. It is now a full-time occupation, supported by the
Home Office and applauded by the Prime Minister. "I see
it as a legacy," says Diana Lamplugh, "Suzy's legacy."

Bruce and Pat Cottrill have devoted their energies to
proving that the murder of their daughter was premeditated, not a random forgettable act, and saw the French
Ambassador last month in an attempt to convince him the
case should be reviewed. Tim Parry's memory is already recorded at the hospital where he died. Their brain-scanning
machine had never been used before, and the doctors asked
Mr Parry whether they could dedicate the scanner to its
first patient. He immediately assented. He has also agreed
to visit Belfast, Dublin and Boston for a *Panorama* programme to coincide with Tim's thirteenth birthday on 1
September. Why? "I want his death to have some meaning
in the context of Ireland, to have it count for something. His
life was pretty well innocent. He was well-liked, he looked
good, he was amiable and gregarious. In fact he was becoming a pretty impressive young man. I cannot let this happen
without making some attempt to keep his name alive."

He will talk to Irish people in the hope of clasping hands.
But there is a danger. "I could not meet anyone who openly
advocated Tim's death or who were callous in their support
for the IRA. That would be too much to bear."

He may also write a book, though he is not yet sure.
Cynics often question the apparent eagerness to "rush"
into print, as if grieving had somehow been contaminated

by vanity and an appetite for publicity. They point out that Dame Jane Gow, widow of the delightful MP Ian Gow who was destroyed by a bomb placed under his car, has never said a word in print anywhere because she regards the whole matter as intensely private. But writing out one's pain and anger can be deeply therapeutic, and at the same time may provide that "monument" which is so desperately needed to help fill the space of absence. Gordon Wilson is in no doubt about it. Writing his book "helped to reconcile me to the facts. My book is a memorial to Marie." He has gone further, and told his story in lectures to packed audiences, pushing himself to the very edge of emotion every time. People come up to him afterwards, many in tears, to say "they have been moved by her, not by me. Even in death, she is doing some good."

The lurking fear is, however, that the writing may unleash a dreadful hatred which can damage rather than heal. Mr Wilson would not permit hatred to rise within him, first because he wanted to protect himself emotionally, second as an intellectual decision not to add to the hatreds already existing. Colin Parry says, "I don't hate the men who did it, because I won't give them the time. They don't enter my mind." Mrs West, however, has been driven by hatred since the day she had to identify her daughter's pathetic remains. It not only informs her book, it is the *raison d'être* behind it. "The beasts still cast their ugly shadow down the years," she writes. Brady and Hindley are called, justifiably, "evil slime", but Mrs West's implacable wrath extends to Myra Hindley's sister, whom she physically attacked, and whose funeral she attended in order to tear to shreds the wreath Myra had sent. For Lord Longford, the "devil's disciple", she has nothing but contempt. When he invited her to lunch, she told him it would choke her.

It may well be that Mrs West can no longer see hatred for the self-destructive emotion which it undoubtedly is. Anger, on the other hand, may be fulfilling and

enhancing. It can supply the energy to find a positive
outlet. Mrs Lamplugh, Mr and Mrs Cottrill, Mr Parry,
even Gordon Wilson, will all admit to anger. It shows
when Colin Parry says, "They should have seen Timmy as
we saw him, broken. It might have opened up their hearts
and made them consider what horrors they exacted upon
a good boy and on a family who did not deserve this. He
was not just a victim. He was a person."

Frédéric Blancke did have one such moment when he
was made to realise that Fiona Jones was not just his
victim, his object, but a person. It was when the judge
in Beauvais invited both Fiona's father and husband to
address the court through an interpreter and describe the
girl they had known. There was a deep, pregnant hush as
their simple and honourable words were translated, and the
murderer sat with his head in his hands. No one was looking
at him, but I glanced across and watched him weep. "It must
surely be possible to reach the hardest of hearts," says Colin
Parry, uncertainly. Yes, I believe it is.

For every one of these injured people forgiveness is,
however, a step too far. Mrs West can no longer recite
the Lord's Prayer with its injunction to forgive those who
trespass against us. Pat Cottrill says Fiona's murderer destroyed her capacity to forgive (and she is a lady of the
sweetest disposition). Diana Lamplugh is certain that she
has no right to forgive Suzy's abductor and murderer,
"only Suzy has that right. He is not worth our distress,
so I can put him on one side." Colin Parry is "deeply
sceptical about people who can say they can forgive a
thing like that. They wish they could, and they want to. I
can't, and yet neither do I want this to force me into having
vicious feelings." Gordon Wilson did not, despite public
perception, use the word "forgive" after his daughter died
at Enniskillen, because forgiveness belongs to God. But
he is still able to recite the Lord's Prayer and feel God's
forgiveness working through him.

Should we take the enquiry one step further, and ask if any good might derive from a meeting between the murderer and the people whose lives he has transformed? Diana Lamplugh is convinced it would not help anyone at all. She knows who killed her daughter, as do the police, although the evidence against him is circumstantial. He sends her messages. She will not play that game, and never will. If she had met him, "I could not have got his face out of my mind." Gordon Wilson did not meet the man who planted the bomb which obliterated his daughter, but he did meet senior representatives of the IRA and came away chastened by their obtuseness and impenetrability.

Once more, the exception is Mrs West, who at one point considered meeting Ian Brady and has been in correspondence with him. Two of his letters are reproduced in facsimile in her book, almost as trophies, as if anticipating the reader's disbelief. She is hard put to justify their correspondence, which she affirms is likely to continue until one or other of them dies, and indicates that she herself is not sure why she does it, except to say that he was "the last person to see Lesley alive". Why, indeed, after what she has endured, should she be called upon to justify herself to *us* in any way at all? It is *her* trouble and *her* pain. But she leaves us with the impression that, of all those who have had to cope with murder, she is the one who has never recovered from it, who is still, in fact, living with it.

The Times, 14 August 1993.

CHAPTER 4

Some Cases

There are murder cases which are remembered throughout the generations, either because they remain unsolved, or were particularly gruesome, or involved people who were already famous for other reasons. The killing of a little boy in the French provinces, Grégory Villemin, is an example of the first; Peter Sutcliffe, the Yorkshire Ripper, illustrates the second; Mrs Harris, schoolteacher and mistress of world-famous dietician, fills the third category. Some overlap into more than one of these divisions, like Jack the Ripper, who operated over a hundred years ago and still makes the skin crawl, because he was especially vicious and was never caught or identified. Again, the case of Lord Lucan's disappearance is remembered both because it is unsolved and because he was a noted gambler; the identity of the murdered victim, however, has completely evaporated from public consciousness. She was called Sandra Rivett.

Other cases reverberate down the years due to their notoriety in leading to miscarriages of justice. John Christie would not be so famous a necrophile were it not for the hanging of Timothy Evans for one of Christie's crimes, an injustice which Ludovic Kennedy worked years to establish; indeed, their address, 10 Rillington Place, is more famous than either of their names, thanks to Kennedy's efforts. Paul Foot has devoted similar energy to proving that those convicted of murdering the paperboy Carl Bridgewater could not possibly be guilty. His work has yet to be rewarded, the Home Office being singularly reluctant to admit error. It took them more than 30 years to advise the Queen to pardon Timothy Evans. Yet another instance of justice going wrong, with disastrous results, is the hanging of Derek Bentley for a murder committed by Christopher Craig. This was the subject of a recent film, *Let Him Have It*.

Murders which retain their interest over the years are naturally submitted to frequent, repetitive scrutiny; there must be almost as many books about Jack the Ripper as there are on Queen Victoria. It is in this way that some of the cases mentioned above have crossed my desk, as books on the subject were sent to me for review, and a selection of those reviews now follows. For good measure, I have included an article which marvelled at the astonishing incidence of murder in one Essex town, and finish with a long account of the Leopold and Loeb case of 1924, famous more for the defence counsel, Clarence Darrow, than for the defendants themselves.

Lord Lucan

Trail of Havoc by Patrick Marnham

On the evening of 7 November 1974, Sandra Rivett, nanny to the children of the Earl and Countess of Lucan, was cruelly battered to death in the basement of the Lucans' house in Belgravia, London, her body stuffed into (of all things) a US mailbag. The Lucans' eldest child, Lady Frances, then ten years old, was upstairs watching television with her mother, who, a few minutes before nine o'clock, went down to see why it was taking Sandra so long to make a pot of tea and was herself attacked on the stairs. Lady Lucan managed to fight the attacker off by grabbing his testicles, and half an hour later, covered in blood, ran into the pub opposite screaming that she had escaped from a murderer.

Lord Lucan left the house shortly afterwards. He visited a friend for a little over an hour, drank a scotch, wrote a couple of letters, and has not been seen since. Lady Lucan later told the police that the man who attacked her was her husband. At an inquest it was concluded that poor Sandra Rivett had been murdered by the seventh Earl of Lucan, since when it has been popularly assumed he is a fugitive from justice. (This was, incidentally, the last time an inquest panel named a murderer; the law has since been amended to prevent a reoccurrence of this anomaly.) There is still a warrant out for Lucan's arrest, but it is superfluous; he has already been "tried" and found guilty in his absence.

One of Patrick Marnham's themes in *Trail of Havoc: In the Steps of Lord Lucan* (Viking) is that the earl could not be found guilty by an impartial jury today. However, to call the book a study of the notorious "Lucan case" would be misleading. The case forms the buffers at each end of the book, while the meat in the middle is an acerbic shaft at the mores of those men who surrounded Lucan and whose values provoked many aberrations in English social life. Marnham, now a writer for *The Independent* in London (indeed, his reports from Paris are one of the best reasons for reading that paper today), contrives (but only just) to control the indignation he feels in contemplating the dramatis personae of his narrative.

But to return to Lucan. Descended from the intemperate soldier whose vanity was one of the chief causes of the infamously disastrous Charge of the Light Brigade in the Crimea, Lord Lucan inherited a fatal propensity to allow grievance to corrode his emotion, and a corresponding belief that action was the only means to satisfy it. He was part of a generation of "cads" and "bounders" who reached manhood in the 1950s and were proud to consider themselves outlaws. One of these, in Marnham's view, was John Aspinall, whose gambling activities led to a change in the law and the explosion of casinos in London in 1960. The most famous and successful of these was Aspinall's own Clermont Club in Berkeley Square, in the basement of which Mark Birley founded his equally famous discotheque, Annabel's. Lucan was a regular punter at the Clermont, as a result of which his inheritance dribbled away.

His marriage also ran into trouble. He and Lady Lucan separated and fought a bitter battle in the courts for the custody of their three children, which was resolved in her favour. Convinced that his wife was unstable almost to the point of madness, and furious that the law should consider her fit to raise a family, he pampered a resentment that poisoned him. He imagined Lady Lucan to be exulting in his defeat. Racked with debts and consumed with an obsessive concern for his children, he pondered whether there might be extralegal ways in which to seek redress.

It is no secret that he wanted his wife dead. He told Aspinall's mother, the late Lady Osborne, as much. But did he try to kill her? The accepted version of events is that he chose to enter the conjugal home (where he no longer lived) on the one evening that the nanny, the hapless Mrs Rivett, would not be there. But she had changed her night off, and Lucan battered her to death in the dark, thinking the victim was Lady Lucan. He became aware of his error when his wife appeared, whereupon he turned his ferocity on her. After a struggle, they went upstairs to the bedroom to talk things over. When she escaped half an hour later, he realised the game was up and fled.

I have never been convinced that after ten years of marriage a man could mistake another woman for his wife, even in the half-light. He would know that the person descending the stairs was not she. Marnham makes this point forcefully, adducing it as one of the principal causes for doubt. Lucan maintained, in one of the letters he wrote the night he disappeared, that he had interrupted a struggle and the intruder made off, but that he knew his wife would be bound to accuse him. This at least accords with the disquieting fact that man and wife spent *half an hour* talking in the bedroom before she flew out of the house; Lady Lucan has never satisfactorily disclosed what was said on that occasion.

Marnham's thesis is that Lucan employed a hit man to do the job for him, and that such a man could easily confuse one woman with the other. This of course does not make Lucan any less guilty, but it does acquit him of the *actus reus* and explain how the wrong corpse could end up stuffed in a mailbag. (That is another mystery: US mailbags are a rare item in England. How did he come by one?) Another book on the case, *Lucan: Not Guilty*, by Sally Moore, which was published in England last fall at about the same time that *Trail of Havoc* appeared there, reaches a different conclusion by a more complex route, suggesting that the murder weapon could have been a truncheon, and the wielder thereof a policeman. In any case, Moore agrees that it is impossible Lucan could have been in the house at the time of Mrs Rivett's death just before nine o'clock; he was seen in Berkeley Square seconds earlier.

Lord Lucan is now either prostrate at the bottom of the English Channel or in hiding somewhere abroad. Every few months there is some dotty "sighting" of him in Upper Greenville or Tierra del Fuego, which the sillier newspapers invariably treat with respect. One place he is not is in the belly of one of Aspinall's tigers (Aspinall is renowned for his pioneering work at two private zoos). Marnham repeats the daft rumour that "Aspinall's tigers were known to be partial to human flesh". Of the more than 300 that he has bred, only one tigress (which, anyway, was imported

from Canada) has proved delinquent, and she showed no
interest in eating her two victims.

Some months after the murder, Dominick Elwes, a
talented portrait artist and wit who was close to the
circle which included Lucan, Aspinall, et al., drew a
picture of a set of gamblers at the Clermont that he sold
to *The Sunday Times* and that was used to accompany an
unfriendly article by James Fox. The fraternity accused him
of betrayal and ostracised him with what Marnham calls
"schoolboy cruelty". Elwes committed suicide. Marnham
then wrote a piece in the iconoclastic satirical magazine
Private Eye entitled "All's Well that Ends Elwes', in which
he mistakenly named the financier Sir James Goldsmith as
being present at a luncheon party given by Aspinall the day
after Lord Lucan disappeared and at which various schemes
to assist Lucan were discussed. Goldsmith consequently not
only brought civil action for libel but also instigated a rare
suit for criminal libel which, had he pursued it, might have
resulted in terms of imprisonment for the editor of the
paper, Richard Ingrams, and for Patrick Marnham himself.
He dropped the case once his point had been made, but was
victorious in several other actions against *Private Eye*.

Why should Goldsmith, at the time eager to own a
London newspaper, be so determined to make enemies in
Fleet Street? Marnham opines that he was gallantly protecting the honour of his friend Lady Falkender, who as Marcia
Williams was Harold Wilson's secretary and who had herself been lashed by the irreverent scorn of *Private Eye*.
Rumours were then flying around that many of Wilson's
friends had shady pasts and that even Wilson himself was
a KGB mole. These stories were leaked to *Private Eye*
by sources within MI5, the British secret service, and as
Spycatcher has since corroborated, they were hatched by
disaffected right-wing civil servants. So we had the odd
spectacle of ultraconservative Jimmy Goldsmith supporting
a socialist government in preventing independent journalists

from investigating whether or not that socialist government was corrupt. The ironies tumbled over one another.

This brings us a long way from Lord Lucan, and even farther from the miserable end of Mrs Rivett. Marnham connects all the threads plausibly enough, assuming that the disparate events reveal a malaise at the heart of English life, where men devoted to an archaic sense of honour and bent on the protection of that privilege which they deem to be their due are ready either to subvert the law or to contort it for selfish ends. but in sheer logic he may have stretched his connections too far. Never mind. *Trail of Havoc* is a splendid piece of sustained analysis. It is avowedly partisan, and doubtless Lucan's friends could answer it, if they chose, with parallel conviction and spirit. That does not detract from the pleasure one derives in reading it.

Vanity Fair, May 1988.

The Yorkshire Ripper

The Streetcleaner: the Yorkshire Ripper case on trial
By Nicole Ward Jouvre

Without any doubt, this is the first serious book on the Yorkshire Ripper case. Of course, there have been other books, but they have been complacent and feeble, content to rehearse details of the murders and investigation with the added spice of some journalistic enquiries into the background of Peter Sutcliffe. As none of the journalists had the imagination to appreciate the significance of what they discovered, Sutcliffe remained a mysterious, feature-less abomination, not a person at all.

Nicole Ward Jouve has brought to the case a fierce, unrelenting intelligence which rejoices in allusions and inferences and nags at every suggested nuance of interpretation until it is made to yield its worth. *The Streetcleaner* is a rich and absorbing book, gripping the reader in awed wonder as it skids from philosophy to linguistics to social history and literature, never losing sight of the power of the central story.

It is also infuriating, because the nature of intuition is to explore unsuspected avenues and sometimes reach appallingly silly conclusions. But this is a risk worth taking; the value lies in the journey. Nicole Ward Jouve is aware of the danger. The French tradition allows speculation in various disciplines, juggling with ideas for the beauty of them and trusting truth to emerge in a series of startling revelations made possible by the clash of unlikely parallels. The English tradition is more banal and solid, it likes its logic to be sequential rather than adventurous.

Nicole Ward Jouve has bags of intuition. The long second section of the book deals with the case mostly from a psychological point of view and her insights here are stimulatingly novel. She depicts Sutcliffe as the wretched product of working-class ideology which makes a model of aggressive maleness and demeans feminine qualities. She has no time for the evolutionary view, that aggression is a genetically inherited characteristic of the male which, when not corrupted, is beneficient.

Young Peter was not aggressive. He loved his mother, hated his brutal and stupid father, might really have been homosexual. Perhaps he was. He married a "nice" girl, not the kind of "slut" his father and brothers went for, as further proof of his identification with mother's ideals. Mother and wife then proved themselves wanting in their absolute purity. Sutcliffe's response was to turn his rage upon prostitutes, blaming them for the sordidness he had glimpsed. He "felled" adversaries (prostitutes) out of love for the two women who mattered to him.

There were many signs of his failed attempt to manufacture maleness in himself. His obsession with machines led him to keep the engine of his favourite motorbike under his bed (typical necrophiliac behaviour, which the author for once misses); the hammers and screwdrivers which he drove into the flesh of his victims were likewise his instruments of manhood. There is even an interesting digression on the metaphors of eating and butchering which litter the vernacular of the northern working class and make Sutcliffe's methods of killing less loathsome to the self-regarding male stud (hence the nickname of "Ripper" which the police half-admiringly bestowed upon the killer).

Sutcliffe's fetish with feet and boots is closely examined and found, astonishingly, to be shared by the detectives; hence their inability to spot the clues it left. Several times Nicole Ward Jouve comes close to suggesting that "society" was in collusion with Sutcliffe, that a miscarriage of justice was necessary to protect the distorted values which the murderer and the prosecutors shared, but even she resists such blinding conclusions. I think she is occasionally caught by surprise when her electric, allusive methods bring her into a maze from which she cannot escape and she must quickly retrace her steps back to the light of sweet reason, leaving the delicious ideas to hover teasingly on the page.

This happens again when, after highly persuasive argument to show Sutcliffe the victim of environment, psychological crippling, semantic confusion and much else besides, she still holds him responsible for what he did, when the logical conclusion would be that he had been programmed to bash women's heads in. At the same time, she accepts his account of being possessed by a genuinely spiritual experience in Bingley cemetery, yet dodges the implications of insanity. The court disputed this and declared him sane. Nicole Ward Jouve does not dispute it, but still wants to chastise him for "choosing" to kill. She cannot really have it both ways, except in the fun of philosophical debate.

When she gets carried away she can be outrageous.
"Being a woman meant you were murderable." "Waste
ground was the place where dead women's bodies belonged." So pervasive is the principle of male supremacy
in the domestic scene that if the wife disturbs it she must
carry the can for whatever happens. Admittedly, these gems
are wrested from their context, but they do illustrate the
traps set by a cavalier attitude towards logic. Never mind.
The book is beautifully written and deeply thoughtful. And
it was time someone applied his/her mind to this dreadful
case.

New Statesman, 7 November 1986.

Mrs Harris

Mrs Harris by Diana Trilling

Until 10 March 1980, Mrs Harris was the unknown headmistress of a posh but equally unknown girls' school in
Virginia. Late that evening she shot and killed her lover
Herman Tarnower, author of a worthless but hugely successful book of dietary advice, and immediately became a
"star", the object of insatiable attention and barely admiss-
ible admiration. After a trial lasting five months, during
which Mrs Harris yielded the spotlight to no one and it
was difficult to recall that a man had died by her agency,
she was found guilty of murder in the second degree and
locked up for a minimum of 15 years. In passing sentence
the judge called her a "brilliant, brilliant woman" and
wished her luck. She has given a television interview since
imprisonment, and the nicely posed photograph on the
back of this book's dustcover was presumably taken after
murder had made her famous.

Why should this be so? On the face of it, the case was perfectly ordinary. Tarnower, in his sixties, had rejected the headmistress's love for the wilder attractions of a pretty, empty-headed young divorcée, and the headmistress was hopping mad. She loaded her gun, drove five hours to see him, and shot him four times. Other people have done as much without exciting the interest of the world's press. Sitting with the three dozen reporters throughout every day of the trial was Diana Trilling, who has now written a thoughtful and stimulating book, far superior to its subject, lucidly explaining why she thinks the case of Mrs Harris holds uncommon fascination for us all.

Mrs Trilling divides her account into three sections. In the first, she clarifies her attitudes before the trial, and admits that she prepared the draft of a book which she subsequently had to scrap, as her perception of Mrs Harris shifted. The long second section covers the trial itself, but mercifully is more than a remorseless presentation of evidence (the reporters were there for that). Mrs Trilling's subtle mind raises questions which both defending and prosecuting counsel would be too dim to understand, follows tangents which illuminate, and suggests general reflections from the particular instance. This is what distinguishes the literary artist from the scribe. Of course, the trial itself makes for a good read, as trials often do, and has its moments of hilarity, as when the detective is asked what he did "with respect to the door" and he replied "Entered through same." But there are no great advocates and no rousing speeches. The trial, for all its celebrity, was essentially provincial.

Mrs Trilling supplies the want with a keen eye for hidden dramas; she observes the defendant constantly and feels the mood of the courtroom. Having begun with contempt for Tarnower, his mean taste and his cruel self-engrossment as revealed in evidence, she comes gradually to despise Mrs

Harris, her prim conventionality and her callous indifference to the result of her act. It is Mrs Harris's respectability
which is on trial. The fact of murder is far from her
consciousness. She is intelligent, well-read, sharp-witted,
ladylike, almost aristocratic. She wears something different
to court every day, has her hair impeccably groomed for
her major role. The very thought of such a splendid person
with a gun in her hand is incongruous. Mrs Trilling discerns
anger, humiliation, social pretension, and doesn't find the
gun at all incongruous. The defence postulates that Mrs
Harris went to her lover's house to commit suicide, and
killed him by mistake in the course of a struggle. As Diana
Trilling drily puts it, she "repeatedly hit the wrong target".

Mrs Harris, nicknamed "Integrity Jean" by her pupils,
manifestly fails to notice that her integrity is compromised
by this pantomime of a trial in which the prosecution
is incompetent and the defence meretricious. At an obviously pre-arranged moment, she bursts into tears and
has her counsel dabbing his eyes as well, sobbing "Look
at me, Jean". She calls him "Joel", and while in the witness
box fighting for her life chats to him as if they were by
the fire at home. When counsel are arguing, as they do
in Hollywood films, the judge says, "Please, fellers, do me
a favour", and Mrs Harris walks over to the press benches
and tells the boys the "truth" which she has not been
allowed to tell in the box.

The last section of this book is a protracted essay upon
matters arising from the case. Mrs Trilling does not agree
with the verdict on the legal grounds that intent to kill was
not proven. But she has a clearer idea of the importance
of the central figure, whom she regards as a character in
fiction, like Anna Karenina or Madame Bovary. Fiction,
she says, has become abstract and no longer deals with
the major themes of the human condition (a proposition
which she does not fully justify – and one wonders what
fiction she has read since Tolstoy and Flaubert). Mrs Harris

belongs to "imaginative writing where ... we learn about character in conflict." She is not the feminist symbol so many idiotic ideologists thought they saw in her, aiming her gun on behalf of women, but a universal victim of the sorry passions which scatter us all. Mrs Harris loved a pathetic man; he ought to have been a great man to deserve her; she loathed him and felt sorry for herself. Well, Mrs Trilling's elegant prose has given her a lasting place in literature. She is now pending an appeal; should her verdict be reversed, she will doubtless become a regular guest on chat shows, and achieve far greater fame than the hapless diet doc whose death made her a star.

The Spectator, 1 May 1982.

The Steinberg case

What Lisa Knew: the truth and lies of the Steinberg Case
by Joyce Johnson

The comatose body of six-year-old Lisa Steinberg was removed by police officers from her parents' grubby two-room flat in Greenwich Village, New York, on a bleak November morning in 1987. The apartment in which she was found was littered with bits of computer equipment entangled with unwashed clothes. In a play-pen in a corner lay her 16-month-old brother, Mitchell, tethered with a rope and stinking of urine; it took three applications of shampoo before his rescuers discovered that his hair was blond. Little Lisa had been so badly beaten that she died shortly afterwards, and her parents were charged with her murder.

The case was sickening, but not, alas, as unusual as it should be. Even the fact that both parents had for years been addicted to "freebasing" cocaine, and apparently had been inhaling it for up to 12 hours while their daughter's inert body lay untended on the bathroom floor, did not, in contemporary New York, render the circumstances unique. The subsequent trial became prime television and newspaper entertainment not because Lisa's fate was so pitiful, but because her parents were presumed to be wealthy professionals and unassailably respectable. Joel Steinberg was a millionaire lawyer. Hedda Nussbaum (they were not married) had been a successful editor of children's books at Random House. Moreover, the children were not their own, nor, it turned out, were they even legally adopted; a physician had persuaded their natural mothers to hand them over to lawyer Steinberg with a view to eventual adoption; but this never took place.

Joyce Johnson has set herself two complementary tasks in this detailed and angry book. First, to explain how people from decent, apparently stable backgrounds could allow their lives to degenerate to a state of incredible brutishness. Second, to show the lamentable frivolity of American courtroom drama.

Hedda Nussbaum was, apparently, a fairly ordinary young woman. Her childhood had been untroubled, her career from university to teaching to publishing unremarkable. She had intelligence, talent, good looks, was fastidious and vain, although, according to Johnson, she showed little emotion and craved sexual enjoyment for its own sake. In common with many young urban women during the 1970s, she indulged in various kinds of therapy as a hobby. Though Miss Johnson does not say as much it is clear that she sees Hedda as a typical schizophrenic without moral perception.

Joel was successful and impressive as a criminal lawyer. He was in fact also a pretentious liar, but that apparently passed unnoticed by a woman who needed to worship a dominant healer. He taught her effective ways of releasing spontaneity, and she responded with slavish adoration. She called him "the giver of love", and they seem to have lived what amounts to a sado-masochistic nightmare. As their behaviour grew less and less reliable, she parted company with Random House and he received fewer briefs.

Joel "acquired" the infant Lisa apparently to bolster his self-image as a father-figure. (Joyce Johnson suggests, without providing evidence, that he may well have been party to the sale of other unwanted babies in order to supplement his already substantial capital.) Lisa evidently adored her new father, but the fretful Hedda grew jealous of her and seems to have succeeded in undermining Joel's affection for her. Johnson has interviewed people who saw Steinberg refuse the child permission to eat for long periods, finally to throw her a sandwich as if to a dog. This viciousness seems to have escalated gradually. Lisa's teachers began to notice that she appeared scruffy and listless; one spotted a suspicious bruise but preferred not to interfere. A neighbour had complained repeatedly to the police about loud quarrelling and other suspect noises in the Steinbergs' apartment, but this had been ascribed to normal marital bickering and the child was not thought to be in danger. Finally, though, she was beaten to death.

All this Johnson describes with mounting disquiet and, it must be said, some imaginative padding. But it is the indignant polemic of her final chapters which lifts *What Lisa Knew* above the merely voyeuristic. Hedda Nussbaum's lawyer, Barry Scheck, made a deal with the prosecution that all charges which Nussbaum faced would be dropped if she agreed to testify against Steinberg. Scheck then portrayed her as a victim, a woman so battered that she dare not break free from her tormentor, and it was this picture which the jury accepted. According to Johnson, Nussbaum was rehearsed for 200 hours in the art of avoiding self-incrimination while appearing numb, vague and suffering. The newspapers accepted this interpretation, but Johnson was, and remains, unconvinced. She details instances of Nussbaum's cruelty to Lisa; points out that she was alone with her for four hours while Steinberg was out at dinner on the night before the child died; that, while Lisa lay unconscious and dying, before telephoning for help she prepared cocaine for Steinberg; she seemed to have felt no affection for the girl and ought, Johnson believes, had natural justice prevailed, to have borne some of the blame.

The contrived theatricality of Johnson's prose – "Perhaps her tragedy was that she lacked the capacity to have one" etc. – often diminishes the force of her arguments. But she does raise important questions, such as why the social services, despite repeated warnings from neighbours, did not properly investigate the Steinberg "family". How had Joel Steinberg been able to assume parenthood without legal authority? And why was Nussbaum's tale not subjected to more energetic scrutiny? Johnson's tentative answer is that the notions of family and motherhood are so sacrosanct in the United States that they cannot be questioned; Hedda Nussbaum had to be seen as a victim, because it was inconceivable that any woman could be so wicked as to collude in the destruction of a child.

Joel Steinberg is now in prison. Hedda Nussbaum lives in seclusion in a country cottage in upstate New York. Mitchell has a new home. Lisa was buried by her natural mother, who had not seen her since she handed her to Steinberg on the day of her birth.

The Times Literary Supplement, March 1990.

Edith Thompson

Criminal Justice: the true story of Edith Thompson
by René Weis

Edith Thompson was hanged for the murder of her husband in 1923, despite the certain knowledge that someone else killed him, despite the lack of evidence implicating her in the deed, despite a public petition urging her reprieve signed by over a million citizens. The manner of her execution was brutal and vile. After four days of hysterical fear at what was to be done to her, she was carried virtually unconscious to the noose and her entrails poured out as she dropped. It was one of those cases which left a mark of shame upon the English judicial process, for Edith assumed that "the law was ultimately bound to protect her, not destroy her", and her impotence in the face of impersonal power which directed she should die must make us all shiver.

René Weis is admittedly partisan. He loathes the notion of capital punishment and makes no secret of the anger it arouses in him. But instead of bombarding the reader with tendentious polemic he tells Edith Thompson's life-story simply and starkly, so that when the appalling final act occurs, our sympathies are so engaged as to share that anger. Mr Weis has had access to Home Office records previously unseen, which enables him, together with other research remarkable for its assiduity, to reconstruct the last months of her life in almost daily detail.

Edith was an intelligent girl with an attractive and lively personality. She loved reading, dancing and the theatre, and though she came from suburban working-class stock she held a responsible position at a city draper's. She married Percy Thompson after a long courtship and without much enthusiasm. A miserable hypochondriac, his successful evasion of war service through persistent (though not serious) ill-health brought upon him the taint of cowardice. Unable to excite his wife's admiration, or even respect, he was given to provoking rows which frequently involved his striking her.

Enter Freddy Bywaters, a handsome lad of 19 and erstwhile schoolfriend of Edith's brother, now walking out with her sister Avis. In Freddy, six years her junior, Edith found the mate for whom her romantic heart yearned. Percy liked him too, and allowed him to move in as a lodger at the Thompson's marital home (bought with Edith's earnings) in Ilford, until one day Freddy intervened to prevent husband ill-treating wife and was asked to leave. By this time, an adulterous liaison was under way, and was pursued throughout the next 16 months with mounting passion.

The lovers could only meet rarely, both because circumspection necessarily controlled their calendar, and because Freddy was a seaman, absent for weeks on end. But they could write to each other. Edith scrupulously destroyed all Freddy's letters, but he kept hers, and these were to prove her undoing. They were unguarded and sentimental, and though I cannot share Mr Weis's assessment of their quality and style, the trial judge's dismissal of them as "gush" was wickedly prejudiced. The letters also fantasised that Percy Thompson's sudden demise, perhaps as the result of a heart attack or poison, would solve all the lovers' problems. Mr Weis maintains that these passages were the product of fevered imagination and that any attempt to take them seriously would be "silly". The jury took a different view.

One evening in October 1922 the Thompsons went to the Criterion Theatre with two friends. They took the Underground back to Liverpool Street and thence a train to Ilford. As they were walking home from the station, a man emerged from the gloom, thrust Edith to the ground and stabbed Percy to death. As the murderer fled the scene, Edith recognised his coat as being Freddy's. From that moment until her last day on earth she could not stop moaning, "Why did he do it?"

The law was in no doubt on this score. He did it because she put him up to it. One of the weaknesses of Mr Weis's study of the case is that he can suggest no other plausible reason, and offers no explanation for Freddy's unexpected and uncharacteristic explosion of violence. They were both arrested and charged with murder, and the subsequent trial was a sensation, attracting crowds to the Old Bailey and the usual hypocritical prurience of the British press, apparently ineradicable.

There was very little the defence could achieve for Freddy, save the obvious inference that the murder was unpremeditated, for he had made no move to conceal the incriminating letters. But Edith's acquittal should have followed from the evidence available. She faced, however, three problems: the remorseless rehearsal of her love letters in court, the revelation of her taste in novels and the hostility of the judge.

Passages in Edith's correspondence appeared ominous when read aloud by counsel. "Be jealous and do something desperate," she wrote. Mr Weis explains that she was afraid of losing Freddy (who had another girlfriend in Australia and had asked if he and Edith could be "only pals"), and she needed to arouse his jealousy, if only by suggestion and innuendo, to keep him. Counsel interpreted the sentence as an instruction to kill. Her final letter, long and amorous, concludes with this: "Don't forget what we talked about in the Tea Room. I'll risk it and try if you will." The prosecution did not hesitate to aver that this was tantamount to a conspiracy to murder. Mr Weis claims that the meeting referred to was an earlier one, not the one which took place the day before the murder, and moreover what they talked about was merely the possibility of Edie finding a job abroad to obviate the continual cat-and-mouse game which degraded their passion. The rest of the correspondence certainly bears this out; there is no specific mention of any collusion, nor of any conspiracy to commit crime.

The letters contained references to poison, notably quinine, which would have to be taken in large doses to produce any harmful effect. The contents of the dead man's stomach contained not the faintest sign of poison, either then or in the past, yet the prosecution successfully reversed the pathologist's report and used it against Edie. Mr Weis reveals that the real reason she could not explain these references to poison was that she was trying to abort. She had carried Freddy's child, and such was the obloquy attached to abortion in 1923 that she would rather stand trial for murder than to admit to such disgrace. It was an instance of the "skewed moral climate of the time".

Bella Donna, a novel by Robert Hitchens in which murder by poison plays a minor role was quoted in court because Edie had read it and discussed it with Freddy. What was not quoted was her letter condemning the heroine and inviting Freddy to share her contempt for such a woman. Another Hitchens novel, *The Fruitful Vine*, was also mentioned as being more of the same stuff. No one in court had read it. The jury was not invited to read either book, yet they both counted against Mrs Thompson.

Thirdly, the judge was palpably antagonistic towards the defendant, at one point pouring scorn on her emotions. "Great love, nonsense," he said, "great and wholesome disgust!" Mr Justice Shearman combined the two most lethal disadvantages to sane judgment – he was stupid, and he was a moralist. The prison chaplain suffered from the same defects, calling upon Mrs Thompson at every visit to "confess". His obtuseness further isolated her.

So keen is Mr Weis to present Edie's case as it should have been presented in court that he understandably errs in the contrary sense, being unwilling to allow that her letters could bear the interpretation given them by counsel. He also attempts to argue from the particular to the general, suggesting that Edith was a victim of something grander than miscarriage of justice, namely the ambivalent attitude towards women which prevailed after the Great War. They had worked for the country in perilous times, now they were a "surplus commodity", they were too easily available and they threatened the moral welfare of our young men. This may be true but its relevance is forced.

Mr Weis succeeds in combining a scrupulous attention to facts, like Zola's *greffier*, with a committed zeal which makes his best pages as taut and gripping as any thriller. Yet his irritating use of the historic present on practically every page suggests he cannot trust himself to get the message across without resort to a stylistic device which should be used sparingly. Still, the effect of this book is to turn one's heart and soul against murder by the State for whatever reason. Those who still glory in the righteousness of capital punishment should read *Criminal Justice* before they resume their baying.

The Spectator, 13 August 1988.

The Molineux Affair

The Molineux Affair by Jane Pejsa

When Jane Pejsa was a little girl growing up in Minneapolis, there lived opposite her a stooped old lady who intrigued her. Her grotesquely hennaed hair, heavily painted face, and voluminous Edwardian garments all betokened dottiness, but she spoke with an elegance of phrase and charm of manner which had long since become obsolete. Most old women have, we are told, a story to tell. This one certainly did, for she had been involved in a murder case at the turn of the century which lasted four years and attracted such attention that crowds fought to get into the courtroom. The Molineux trails had long since been forgotten, but nobody knew that Blanche Molineux was still alive, stranded half a century beyond her time, and holed up in a small room in Minneapolis with tatty curtains and cloths hung over the lamps.

Jane's mother persuaded the old lady to write down what she could remember of the trials and the events which preceded them, and she inherited these diaries when Blanche died, unnoticed, in 1954. In the years since, Jane has consulted old newspapers and dug out court transcripts to complement and support Blanche's account, so that now she is able to tell her story in full. This, briefly, is what it amounts to.

As Blanche Chesebrough she had been a pretty young woman with ambitions to become an operatic soprano. She studied music to this end, but her means were insufficient, as she belonged to what taxi-drivers sometimes call the lower-middle-classes. Then she met dashing, handsome, rich, young man-about-town Roland Molineux, son of the famous and respected Civil War General Edward Molineux. To make it even more romantic, the meeting took place on a yacht. For Roland, though a champion on the parallel bars, with a chest and shoulders to make any girl faint and a waist a ballet-dancer might envy, was sadly not easily tumescent. Life is very unjust that way.

Roland courted Blanche notwithstanding (pardon the pun) his difficulties, and introduced her to his best friend Henry Barnet. Now Henry had a pot belly and a double chin, was no bristling Apollo, but could make a girl happy without embarrassing effort. Blanche allowed herself to be seduced by Henry while still officially engaged to Roland. As Miss Pejsa puts it, with I think detectable prurience, "she knew what she might expect this night, and she was more than ready for it."

All that was great fun, but she still wanted to marry Roland because he had the money, the position, the nice house, etc, and all Henry had was, well, the confidence. Roland and Henry both belonged to the Knickerbocker Club in New York, and word soon got round that the pretty Miss Chesebrough was friendly with both gentlemen. Then Henry suddenly fell ill and died of a mysterious malady. Weeks later, Roland and Blanche were married.

Roland had an enemy at the Knickerbocker Club, one Harry Cornish, athletic director, who was coarse and vulgar while Roland was refined and smooth. They squabbled, and to Roland's chagrin the house committee took Cornish's side, so Roland promptly resigned. Cornish's aunt, Mrs Adams, was then seized by violent convulsions and she too died of a mysterious malady. This time a post-mortem examination revealed the cause of death to be poison by cyanide of mercury. The poison was contained in a phial of powder sent anonymously to Harry Cornish, obviously the intended victim. Henry Barnet's body was then exhumed and studied: cyanide poisoning again.

The murderer had ordered the poison to be delivered to a private numbered letter-box before posting it on to his victims. Diligent detective work showed that the same man had previously written to buy a cure for male impotence. At the inquest on Mrs Adams, Roland Molineux was identified as the culprit, his motives being jealousy in the first instance, hatred in the second. He was arrested and indicted for murder.

His subsequent trial, appeal, and retrial were sensational for the ever-delightful spectacle of seeing the posh suffer, as Molineux was upper crust by New York standards, and Americans, however much they may protest the contrary, have a hierarchy of class which a pneumatic drill could not dent. The press gleefully picked upon Blanche Molineux's amorous ditherings and Roland's ineptitude in lust with an indifference alike to justice and good manners. *Plus ça change.* The trial also provided one of those irresistible courtroom dramas which actors cannot wait to get their hands on. The prosecuting attorney, James Osborne, deserved full marks for meretricous oratory and histrionic flourish. Miss Pejsa must be commended for unearthing these entertaining records, which provide the best chapters of her book, and will doubtless offer the best scenes of the presumably inevitable film.

If there is a film, it will at least spare us some unimaginative prose. To describe a town in New Jersey as "short on greenery and long on fumes" is ugly. Blanche too often throws herself on the bed to sob. And when a paragraph begins, "Days became weeks and suddenly weeks were months as December became January and January slipped into February", one feels one has spent too much of one's life gawping at words and one wants one's Desert Island to be, please, totally devoid of books. But there is one happy howler which brings back a smile: "shades of *déja vous*", writes Miss Pejsa with the assurance of a polyglot.

It is a good story, and Jane Pejsa organises it well. But it's not all that important. It is an awkward fact that though there are many attics and dungeons hiding papers never before seen by anyone, the papers can still be ordinary. Roland Molineux was found guilty on circumstantial evidence alone, then acquitted at his second trial. He ended his days in a hospital for the insane, as cerebral syphilis gradually reduced him to a raving lunatic. The lawyers grew fat and famous and died. The newspapers passed on to other matters. Blanche Molineux disappeared from view and was never heard of again. Until, 50 years later, Jane Pejsa's mother became a neighbour of an eccentric old lady with an amazing story to tell . . .

The Literary Review, May 1988.

Joseph Bowne Elwell

The Slaying of Joseph Browne Elwell
by Jonathan Goodman

What is good about this book is the author's meticulous method in knitting together the confusing and contradictory details of an unsolved murder case in 1920. If you are going to embark on this kind of retrospective investigation it is essential to be thorough, and Mr Goodman, as he has shown before, is no slouch. He has managed to reconstruct events in the hours before and after the death of his subject with such vivid control that it might have happened yesterday.

The victim, Joseph Bowne Elwell, was quite famous in his day. Known as the Wizard of Whist, he came from modest beginnings to ingratiate himself with the rich socialites of New York and Rhode Island by teaching them how to play the fashionable new game of bridge. Indeed, he is part of the history of bridge, by virtue of his having taught W.K. Vanderbilt, who went on to develop contract bridge. Elwell wrote many popular handbooks to the game and made himself wealthy enough to dabble in property speculation and various lucrative investments, including racehorse ownership. He married an ambitious but rather unpleasant woman and they had one son before drifting apart. By 1920 he was *persona grata* everywhere, lived in a handsome townhouse, dined in the most expensive places.

One June evening, Elwell dined with four friends at the Ritz-Carlton, then took them all to a night-club above the New Amsterdam Theatre. They left in the early hours, Elwell taking a cab home alone. When his housekeeper arrived the next morning, she found him with a letter in his hand, three more on the floor by his feet, and a bullet-hole in his head. It looked as if he had just begun to open the mail when someone simply shot him and walked away. There was no sign of struggle or surprise. Elwell probably knew his assailant.

What followed in the weeks afterwards was crudely farcical. The detectives charged with the case were not only inept but idiotic, changing their minds from day to day and arguing with one another. It was even seriously suggested the crime could be suicide, though the absence of a gun might make anyone but a New York cop wonder how Elwell contrived to get rid of the weapon after clawing out his own brains. The *New York Times* charitably pointed out that the District Attorney was under no obligation to be a detective of genius. There were no real clues, but what little certainty existed was smothered by uninhibited press speculation, the bane of an inquisitive society. Ouija boards and obscure countesses made their appearance for a day, as did a bright spark who chastised police for not taking a photograph of the victim's eyes, wherein would lie the image of the last object they saw.

Goodman examines all the nonsense that was bruited (much of it so irrelevant that it could have been neglected without harm), before coming up with his own identification of the murderer in the penultimate chapter. It is fair to suspect that he wants to bombard the reader with complexity the better to demonstrate the clarity of his own solution once the dross has been swept away.

It would, of course, be wrong to reveal this solution, but justifiable to point out that it relies more on intuition than evidence. The reader must determine for himself whether it was worth waiting for.

In the meantime, he will have to struggle through some of the most viscous prose I have ever come across. Mr Goodman is not exactly someone who cannot write, but someone who tries too hard, who grapples with words as if he has to beat them. What is one to make of phrases like "slightly less unonerous", "a become-anonymous *negligée*", "gossip columnists' unanimous un-doubtednesses", "uneuphemistic", or "which would have increased only extremely"? Does one forgive the invention of new verbs, such as "to unconcentrate"? Is one meant to admire this as stylistic and syntactical freedom? Or is it the ungainly result of an attempt to be clever? Mr Goodman is allergic to the juxtaposition of adjective with the noun it is meant to qualify; hence "breathtakingly beautiful of tresses", "cacophonous of speculation", "bisexual of entries" (that's an address book), and so on – there are dozens of them. Such is the cumulative effect of this linguistic toffee that tolerance folds up half way through and one is driven to the conclusion that the writing is a load of old rubbish.

Form matters as much as content, possibly even more so in the end. A dull subject can be invested with seductive interest when presented in clear harmonious prose (as, for example, Bertrand Russell on education or Iain Moncreiffe on heredity). Conversely, a bright subject may be crippled by ugly language. The Elwell case provides material for a good book, but if you let someone like Jonathan Goodman on it, you need a firm editor to stop him ruining it.

The Literary Review, May 1987.

Charlie Richardson

My Manor by Charlie Richardson

It is rare for an author to reveal himself as guilelessly as this one. Charlie Richardson, working "with" Bob Long and, presumably, a tape-recorder, is anxious to present himself as one who knew how the world worked at the age of eight and conquered it before puberty. "Authority", he says, "has no power unless you give it recognition." Not for Charlie the humiliation of being told what to do; he had wings, he wanted to "gorge" himself on life, and would allow nobody to restrict him. So what did he do? He became a petty and rather despicable bully and ended up spending the better part of his manhood in prison.

The strain of the pitiful throughout this tawdry book is pervasive. Richardson is proud of himself for insulting an admittedly bovine sergeant-major who dared to yell at him when he was conscripted, and one is dumb with wonder that he could still be so adolescent. He does not dissemble. Power was what he hungered for, and the only route to power for a surburban London boy with the wrong accent and a gargantuan chip on his shoulder was through bone-headed indifference to a beating and an icy determination to solicit trust and then betray it. If people trust you completely, "your power is so great that you own them". Thus Charlie nourished his sense of invincibility, and anyone who threatened to dilute it could always be slapped about a bit. He still does not see that he was so afraid of accepting others as equals that he effectively denied himself the opportunity to mature.

What he did instead was to embark upon a life of crime. Extortion from other boys, stealing cars, pinching lead from roofs and flogging it to fences, nothing was too negative for this warped kid who thought he was riding high. By the age of 17 he was experienced in fraud and had already spent time inside, as had his father before him. Charlie started a business in scrap-metal dealing, mostly stolen, and kept the cops happy with weekly pay-offs. The Metropolitan Police ran the most efficient protection racket in London, he assures us, and there is little reason to disbelieve him. As a businessman with "unorthodox" methods (like employing arsonists), he had to protect his interests and gathered round him some pretty sordid friends. He does not like the word "gang", as that sounds rather childish. He would prefer "associates". As for himself, he was a "streetfighting artful dodger" who grew into an "entrepreneur". I would prefer "thug". The violence of the man is transparent in the menace of his language. "I nutted him on the bridge of his nose which I felt crumble under my head."

An interest in mining took Charlie to South Africa, where they really knew how to treat a man – best hotel rooms and as much lobster thermidor as his deprived soul could crave. The South Africans did not seem to mind his showing off and he even found his best-ever "bint" there, but the merry-go-round came to an abrupt halt when he and his friends were arrested on various charges, including Grievous Bodily Harm, and put before the public in a sensational trial at the Old Bailey in 1967. He was, briefly, as famous as the Krays, but the bitterness he feels (he was, of course, framed) against his 25-year sentence and the duplicity of everyone except Charlie Richardson informs this book from the opening page and goes on festering until the last.

His only defence now is what Macaulay called "the sarcasms which modish vice likes to dart at obsolete virtue". The jury were "soggy grey people" or "sad grey little people with sad grey little lives". The press benches were full of "flea-ridden hacks" or "dandruff, pot bellies and spotty fat arses". As for the judge, the gentle and wise Fred Lawton, nothing will contain Richardson's spleen, except my resistance to quote. Nor is nastiness a new characteristic, discovered in adversity. As a little boy he found himself facing a nicely scrubbed child in a train: "I looked at the little pink baby pig opposite and I knew I could kick his head in and enjoy the bubbling tears." This pathetic man has been poisoned by hatred all his life. His favourite word is "shit" (as in "beat the shit out of"), and his scabrous account of a worthless existence is not even rescued by humour or irony. I only laughed once, when Richardson described the New York Mafia as "nice people, interesting and adventurous and very polite".

Charlie is certain he was respected by the people in his "manor"; I grew up in Camberwell and remember that he aroused there as much awe as a scorpion. Heaven knows why this book was published. The sooner it is pulped the better.

The Spectator, May 1991.

Little Grégory Villemin

Little Grégory by Charles Penwarden

The unsolved murder of four-year-old Grégory Villemin on 16 October 1984 makes the heart break with pity, for he was almost certainly the victim of those wretched emotions which disfigure adult life – envy, jealousy, revenge – from the effects of which he ought to have been protected. His body was found floating in the River Vologne three hours after his mother had reported him missing. She had brought him home from school and last saw him playing with bucket and spade on a mound of gravel outside the house.

Grégory had not struggled. His body was at peace, as if sleeping. Perhaps he knew his killer well. It would not have been difficult in a village where everyone was related to some degree or other to everyone else. Or he might have been sedated. In the absence of any adequate pathological examination, this can never be verified. From his birth, his parents, Jean-Marie and Christine, had been subjected to vicious anonymous letters and telephone calls from someone calling himself The Crow, threatening all manner of retribution for Jean-Marie's modest success in life. Known as "the Chief", Jean-Marie had antagonised the neighbours by getting richer than them and making sure that they knew it. He had married a girl from outside the region, who was deemed to have airs. They had to be punished.

The letter which announced Grégory's abduction must count among the nastiest manifestations of evil ever penned. "I hope you die of sorrow, chief," it said. "Not all your money can give you back your son. This is my revenge, poor fool." At the funeral, Christine's grief was awful to behold; she eventually fainted. Jean-Marie broke his wrist slamming it against a wall in frustrated anger, an indication, perhaps, of the raw, primitive emotions which governed life in his untutored backwater. What happened in the next few years was grimmer than any Balzac tale, more malign then the selfish manoeuvres of a François Mauriac character. Indeed, one is reminded of Mauriac's *Le Noeud de Vipères* as the Villemin family, over 100 of them, clam up in their determination to preserve their own poison.

The first suspect was the boy's uncle. The police were so sure of their man that they forgot some essential rules of enquiry which might have averted the nauseating farce which ensued. The uncle had an unassailable alibi. Then suspicion fell upon the father's first cousin, Bernard Laroche, who was shopped by his sister-in-law, a 15-year-old half-wit. She subsequently retracted her statement, probably under family pressure, but it was too late to save Bernard, who was murdered in front of his wife and son by a furious Jean-Marie. Yet more bizarrely, Grégory's mother, Christine, was then arrested and charged with the murder of her own son. It seemed she had been spotted posting a letter at the time The Crow would have sent his last letter to the Villemins; that her telephone bills had increased alarmingly in volume at the very time The Crow had been making his calls; that her handwriting more resembled The Crow's semi-literate script than did anyone else's.

By this time there was no one in France who did not have an opinion on the case, and few who did not despise Christine Villemin with a vicious glee. Marguerite Duras, who should have known better, joined the noisome chorus with a squalid piece of literary interference – in which she famously described the murder as *"forcément sublime"*. All this, remark, before the faintest whisper of any trial.

One of the virtues of this book is to clarify the ways of French jurisprudence, wherein the very verb used to indict, *inculper*, carries within it the supposition of guilt, and the *juge d'instruction* is charged with gathering sufficient evidence to allow him an "intimate conviction" of a person's guilt. This particular judge, 33 years old when he began his enquiry, made an unholy mess of it. One example: a key witness saw a blue bundle floating in the river at 5.30 p.m. It was assumed to have been the little boy, who wore a blue anorak. Not until five years later was the witness shown the anorak, upon which she emphatically declared that it was not what she has seen at all. It is now thought the murder was committed much later, by which time Christine was surrounded by police and neighbours searching for their child. The agony this woman has suffered could have been avoided by less sloppy investigation at the start.

Penwarden's book is more detailed than any account I have yet seen, but its gasping style lacks the gravity which the case merits. Ludovic Kennedy would know better how much weight to allow each link in the labyrinthine tale; and besides, it might test his oft-repeated faith in the French system. Meanwhile, The Crow has succeeded in his avowed aim to destroy the lives of Jean-Marie and Christine Villemin, who, both released from custody, are attempting a new anonymous life in a town far away from the scene of their awesome tragedy, while a new *juge* with more experience has hinted at the eventual revelation of a suppurating conspiracy.

The Listener, 9 August 1990.

The Krays

Reg and Ron Kray: Our Story with Fred Dinenage

The Kray twins love being famous. Reg coyly admits he is something of a folk hero to the younger cons, and is irritated by people who *claim* acquaintance with them when he knows for certain they have never met.

No doubt film stars are pestered in like fashion. It is burdensome to be a hero, after all. Ron has few misgivings about his notoriety, rejoicing in the observation that when he and his brother appeared in the dock at the Old Bailey, they were "big box office". He would not dream of disdaining the fans.

But what is this pair famous *for*? Have they built, written, studied, achieved anything? Have they contributed towards our knowledge of the human condition, or served the community with some laudible entertainment? Not a bit of it.

They are known simply because for years they were big-headed but small-minded crooks who befouled the London scene with their squalid protection rackets and gruesome manners, until they were sent down in 1969 for a minimum of 30 years, having been convicted of vicious, moronic murders. It is dismal enough to reflect that we all know who they are, worse still that a publisher should think there is sufficient interest in their crimes to warrant giving the brothers an opportunity to parade themselves yet again.

John Pearson wrote an admirable account of their "careers" years ago. What the Krays now add, each having alternate chapters presumably tape-recorded by Mr Dinenage, is a vainglorious, occasionally repellent, display of pride masquerading as honesty. Each plumes himself with having been a "right little bastard" as a child growing up in a tough neighbourhood, and each claims he was afraid of no one.

They evolved quite naturally into gangsters, because they lacked the brains or courage for anything else, and they speak openly of their "reign" in London's nauseous underworld. Each justifies the murder he committed by the (uncontested) villainy of the victim, but the pleasure they derived from the act is apparent. Ron says he "felt fucking marvellous" and that "everybody looked at me with a new respect" after he had shot Cornell through the forehead. He still thinks about it, and enjoys it every time.

The pathetic arrogance of these two is breathtaking, their threatening tone (which they would not have the gumption to disguise) ludicrous in the circumstances. I am prepared to

admit they frighten me enough – I would certainly not want
to meet either of them alone. But then I would not want to
meet them at all; they are simply not interesting. It is beyond
them to understand that gangsters are banal and boring.

A criminal psychiatrist might find something of value
behind the boastfulness. It is significant they tend to blame
everyone else for their misfortune – the police, other gangs,
their cronies. They were too soft, too trusting, the world is
made of shits who let them down.

This is commonly the plea of men who fail to make
their mark on merit, and the Krays are failures above all
else. Their abject courtship of show-business personalities
who fluttered around the semi-bright lights of Swinging
London demonstrates a desire to shine by proxy. There is
a certain child-like innocence in their inability to see themselves clearly even now. They never reached maturity, but
remained the "right little bastards" they had been as kids.

Reg and Ron both deplore the violence which disfigures
our TV screens today, and wonder how modern children
will escape the contamination. If they were still around,
says Reg, the streets would be safer, there would be less
mugging and we could leave our front doors open as we
used to. Their way with muggers would be to "smack them
in the gob" (Ron's expression). To his credit, Reg is a trifle
shamefaced by his own moral preaching.

It would be difficult to argue against one point they
make, which is that Blunt sent far more people to their
doom, and dispassionately, yet was permitted to hold his
head high for years. Justice is not, it is true, applied justly.
But I would not want it to be applied by people like this.

The Sunday Telegraph, 18 September 1988.

Jeffrey Dahmer, during his trial. *(Press Association)*

Dennis Nilsen, five years before he committed his first murder. (*Press Association*)

Carl Stottor, photographed some years after Nilsen's attack. (*Roger Hutchings/ The Observer*)

Diana Lamplugh, mother of missing estate agent Suzy Lamplugh, launching the Missing Persons' Help Line in Bristol. *(PA Picture by Barry Batchelor)*

Fiona Jones on her wedding day, with her mother Mrs Cottrill. *(Reproduced by kind permission of Mr and Mrs Cottrill)*

Colin and Wendy Parry, outside Warrington General Hospital. (*PA Picture by Malcolm Croft*)

Derek Bentley, who was hanged for his part in the murder of a Police Constable. *(Popperfoto)*

Christine Villemin was charged with murdering her son Gregory (*inset*), found drowned in Vologne River. *(AFP/Feferberg)*

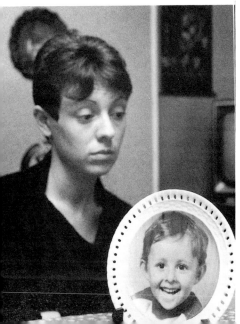

Danish-born financier, Claus von Bülow at the trial where he was acquitted of attempting to murder his wife with insulin injections. *(Popperfoto)*

Sunny von Bülow, the wife of Claus von Bülow. *(Popperfoto)*

Mrs Edith Thompson and Frederick Bywaters, both hanged for the murder of Mr Thompson. *(Popperfoto)*

Nathan Leopold and Richard Loeb laughing during the trial in which they are charged with the kidnapping and murdering of 14-year-old Bobby Franks. *(Popperfoto)*

Sir Anthony Hopkins, demonstrating the success of SILENCE OF THE LAMBS. *(Rex Features photo by Richard Young)*

Derek Bentley

Scapegoat by John Parris

Derek Bentley, an illiterate half-wit prone to epilepsy, was hanged for murder in 1953 after a trial attended by much sensational publicity, firstly because he was only 18 years old, and secondly because it was never suggested that he had killed anyone. Nearly 40 years later, after books by H. Montgomery Hyde, David Yallop and others, as well as a television programme, the case can still excite emotions, especially with regard to the manner in which Lord Chief Justice Goddard conducted the trial. Most people in the judiciary continue to maintain that Goddard was scrupulously fair. A few, of whom Bernard Levin is the most notable, insist he was viciously prejudiced against the defendants. This new book, by the only surviving barrister in the case, is almost embarrassingly shrill in its hatred and contempt for Goddard, depicting him as a bigoted and perverted old lecher who derived improper satisfaction when delivering the death sentence.

The bare bones of the case are simple enough. Bentley and his friend Christopher Craig set out to burgle a butcher's shop in Croydon. They were intercepted by police, who pursued them to the roof of a warehouse where Bentley was apprehended and held by an officer. After this, another officer was shot and killed, presumably by Craig, who was armed (though no ballistic evidence was ever presented to demonstrate that the bullet which killed PC Miles came from Craig's gun – there were other guns on the roof held by other police officers). As Craig was only 16, he could not be hanged, but was detained for some years and now lives in the country. The author of this book was Craig's counsel.

Bentley was hanged because it was held that he was party to the "joint venture" whose purpose continued even after his arrest and detention on the roof and despite his having no gun. He did have a knuckleduster, which might indicate a shared purpose to resist arrest. What really secured his conviction were his words to Craig just before the shot was fired –"Let him have it, Chris." Some authors have contested that this could be interpreted as an imprecation to Craig to surrender the weapon. John Parris now goes further and doubts that the words were said at all.

He posits the theory that the police, determined that somebody should pay for the death of their colleague, pored over law books and found a precedent in the case of R. v. Appleby, in which the very same words were uttered by another defendant in a similar situation; they lifted these words from the former case and fraudulently placed them in Bentley's mouth. Certainly, there was no independent corroboration that these words were used, apart from the evidence of three policemen. Certainly, also, we now know all too well that the police are capable of perjury, though in the innocent mood of 1953 such a notion was deemed all but impossible. Bentley could not write his name, so somebody else signed his statement couched in typical police jargon, which even a literate youth would not have used. It is, however, fanciful to imagine coppers leafing through law books, beside which there are hundreds of other precedents relevant to "joint venture" which they might have consulted, whereas Parris gives the impression that R. v. Appleby is the only one.

The imputation that Lord Goddard wanted at all costs to see somebody hang for his personal satisfaction is a serious one. It seems that even as a small boy he would entertain his school friends by reciting the legal formula for the death penalty. There is plenty of evidence in *Hansard* that his eagerness to reintroduce flogging was suspiciously extreme. It is also on record that, in his summing-up in the Craig/Bentley trial, he devoted only one sentence to the case for Bentley's defence. Mr Parris tells us that Goddard lost his temper when a juryman asked to see an exhibit which

Goddard thought irrelevant (because it pointed towards mitigation), and smashed the knuckleduster on his desk, causing damage which may still be seen today.

The jury recommended mercy for Bentley. Had the judge supported them, the Home Secretary, David Maxwell Fyfe, would have been bound to take notice. Indeed, it has always been believed in legal circles that Goddard did recommend that Bentley should not hang. Parris says that the Home Secretary told him personally (as part of a delegation urging the Royal Prerogative) that Goddard had both verbally and in writing insisted that the death penalty be carried out. If this be true, then Goddard stands condemned of hypocrisy. If it is not true, then it is the most contemptible slur upon the man's memory. We cannot check, as the records have been locked away until the year 2047, on the grounds that they contain "sensitive material".

As one would expect of a former member of the Bar, Parris writes with commendable clarity and precision, and his analysis of the issues is just. Unfortunately, he also writes in an astonishingly vituperative spirit, which suggests he has several axes to grind, and forfeits the reader's trust. To call somebody one does not like a bastard indicates, at the least, a lack of control, and when he finally explodes with the verdict that judges are "at heart all fascists (who) believe in order over justice", then we may legitimately question his judgement.

The Spectator, 6 July 1991.

Carl Bridgewater

Murder at the Farm: who killed Carl Bridgewater?
by Paul Foot

By the time this review appears, new evidence will have emerged to demonstrate still further the weakness of the case against Michael Hickey, convicted, with two others, of the murder of newspaper boy Carl Bridgewater on 19 September 1978. A fellow prisoner, Brian Sinton, testified that while on remand Hickey had confessed to the murder as they shared a shower. He now says he made it all up on the advice of a prison officer in return for better treatment by the screws. Had Paul Foot been able to trace Mr Sinton (who had changed his name) he would have been able to add this intelligence to his already massive file. But it need only have occupied a paragraph, for Foot's work on the case has been so comprehensive that he has a dozen far more compelling reasons to suggest that the men serving life imprisonment for that foul killing are entirely innocent.

Carl Bridgewater was blasted by a shotgun because he delivered a newspaper at Yew Tree Farm while burglars were doing the place over. The four men who stood trial for the crime were Vincent Hickey, his cousin Michael Hickey, James Robinson and Pat Molloy. Three were convicted of murder, while Molloy was found guilty of manslaughter largely because it was his confession, written by police officers and signed by him, which implicated the other three.

Let us be Devil's Advocate for a moment. Paul Foot is proselytiser by nature, and this is a polemical work designed to persuade the reader to the author's point of view; it therefore tends to minimise evidence which runs counter to that view. Two examples: the boy's bicycle had been trodden on exactly as one of the defendants, Pat Molloy, said it had been in his rush to escape from the scene, and the drawers of the chest in an upstairs bedroom had been stacked neatly after searching, just as Molloy said they had been. Molloy later claimed that his confession had been extracted under relentless harsh questioning, which it probably had, that he had not been at the farm at all. These two awkward corroborations of the truth are mentioned briefly by Foot, then allowed to disappear.

Again, the four men were all rogues in varying degrees, and had been involved in other criminal offences. No one could pretend their souls were pure, and it was easy to believe them capable of real wickedness.

Thirdly, the verdicts were unanimous and firm, and they have been upheld by subsequent Home Office enquiries conducted in secret.

Having said that, Paul Foot has assembled a dossier of facts which certainly point to a miscarriage of justice. To call his research "painstaking" would be feeble, grabbing at a word to denote toil and commitment, whereas his pursuit of detail to build up his case is simply more thorough than anything I have encountered in a book of this kind. At the very least, the men should not have been convicted on the evidence presented in court, which was astonishingly thin considering the gravity of the charges. How, then, did it happen?

Foot is cautious in his choice of words, but it is obvious he thinks the police were dishonest and the judge incompetent. Instances of misdirection to the jury and of questionable police behaviour are too numerous to list in a review, but among the telling conclusions which Foot draws are:

1) no witness ever saw the four men together. The Hickeys were hardly acquainted with the other two, and nobody saw them at the scene of the crime. Robinson was identified as the man three witnesses had separately noticed at Yew Tree Farm, but against all the rules they made their identifications on reflection afterwards, not at the parade. It was Robinson's head of hair which alerted them. At the

time of the crime, however, Robinson had been virtually
bald, having shaved his scalp three weeks before.
2) the car which the murderer(s) used and which was seen
parked at the farm was never traced. Hickey had had a
similar vehicle, but it had been scrapped long before the
events in question.
3) none of the items stolen in the course of the robbery has
ever been found.
4) the four men were in two separate pubs 20 miles from
the farm until three o'clock; they could not have met up and
made the journey in time for Carl's death. Besides which,
5) all four were elsewhere when the crime was committed.
Witnesses who could establish their alibis, which could
easily be corroborated by others, were not called. One was
even withdrawn at the last minute because counsel for the
Crown admitted there was a "grave risk" she might prove
the defendant could not have been at the farm.
6) police officers invented statements and promised to leave
witnesses alone if they would sign them.
7) no forensic evidence was ever discovered. Not a finger-
print or tyre mark could be produced. Direct evidence,
opposed to "verbals", was nonexistant.
8) Robinson did possess a shotgun, and led police to where
it was concealed. It could not, however, have fired the shot
which killed Carl Bridgewater. The murder weapon was
never found.

There is much more. Perhaps one is naive to be seduced
by the passion of the proselytiser, and Foot's charges might
all be demolished by a proper investigation. If so, I cannot
wait to read it. The three surviving defendants (Molloy died
in prison) have all rigorously protested their innocence
ever since. Of course, guilty men often do, but the prison
grapevine, which one may choose to heed or not, supports
them, and prisoners are usually fine arbiters in such matters.
Additionally, the *on dit* inside names the real murderer. So,
somewhat riskily, does Paul Foot.

Still, one is not here to determine whether or not Mr Foot is right. One hopes another review of the case might do that. Our question must be, is this a good book? I found it totally absorbing. Even if I did not have to earn my pennies, I should have devoured every word. Foot organises his material with a scrupulously steady mind. He does not screech or whine, but progresses purposefully from paragraph to paragraph, each closely reasoned and written with care. So-called "investigative" journalism often hides muddy exploitation. Paul Foot has given it a new dignity in this brilliant piece of work.

The Literary Review, November 1986.

Murders in Coggeshall

About six miles from Braintree in Essex, on the Colchester road, lies one of the most beautiful small towns in England. Coggeshall is a place built with a painter's eye for harmony, balance and gentle colour. It is a delight to walk its streets and gaze at its houses, few of which have ambitions above a couple of storeys. One, built by the town's clothier Thomas Paycocke in 1500, and quite properly known as Paycocke's House, is among the finest half-timbered houses in the country, while the local pub, the Woolpack Inn, is equally picturesque. Next to the Inn is St Peter ad Vincula, an imposing Gothic church which boasts a very unusual monument to one Mary Honywood; at her death in 1620 she was mourned by 367 living descendants.

Coggeshall (or Great Coggeshall as it ought accurately to be called) is very old. Roman coins and tiles, urns, human bones, evidence of a substantial Roman house, and some sinister sacrificing dishes, have all been found here. The prevailing tone of the town is, however, sixteenth century and slightly soporific. Little seems to happen. In keeping with its genteel antiquity, Coggeshall is the natural home for a score of antique shops, mostly cosy and cluttered but occasionally large and expensive.

This could be E.F. Benson country, where ladies meet for tea and chatter, where a new arrival is scrutinised for her little faults and praised for her charitable work with the church, where gossip outside the butcher's shop is about upstarts and temporary outcasts. Except that it isn't. P.D. James would be more appropriate a resident than E.F. Benson, for the gossip is more likely to be about murder and death.

Go down the road to the street corner in the centre of town and see a low, green building called Peter Langan's Restaurant. Langan was that overbearing and irascible drunk, as famous for his disgusting manners as for his good food, who set fire to himself in front of his wife in 1989. Or there is the house called Bouchiers Grange, where lived an arable farmer called Jimmy Bell. In 1986 he murdered his beautiful young wife before turning the shotgun to his own chest and blasting himself into oblivion.

One of the most respected and experienced dealers in antiques, as well as one of the richest, was Wilfred Bull. A world expert on ivory carvings, he shot his wife Patsy in 1985 in their warehouse, surrounded by his antiques, then hid the gun under the floorboards. He is currently serving a life sentence for her murder. And what about that lovely little pub we mentioned next to the church – the Woolpack Inn? Surely that rings a bell? This is the last place to see Diane Jones alive in 1983. Her body was found three months later, and her husband questioned at inordinate length. Dr Jones was never charged, but the relentless appetite of publicity chewed him up for years afterwards. Decidedly, it is murder and suicide that have put Coggeshall on the map in the late twentieth century, not antiques or architecture. Residents cannot deny there is something distinctly odd about so many violent deaths occurring among such a small population.

A local shopkeeper gave voice to a general apprehension that most of the townfolk prefer to conceal. "There is something here which changes personalities," he said. Two taxi-drivers in Chelmsford refused to drive to Coggeshall, and the third admitted that he found the place "attractive but weird – I don't feel comfortable there." Are they not all being a trifle over-imaginative? Surely the incidence of crime stretches way beyond the confines of this little town to embrace most of Essex. Coggeshall does seem to be at the epicentre in some indefinable way. Stories cross and interweave, and often bring one back to the town with a logic which is nicely hidden. Consider this: Coggeshall Abbey was founded by King Stephen and Queen Maud in the twelfth century, and in the late thirteenth century was inhabited by a famous abbot called William de Tolleshunt. Today, a few miles away, is a lovely Regency village named after him, a village which claims one of the only original maypoles left in the country. It is called Tolleshunt d'Arcy, and it was here in 1985 that Jeremy Bamber murdered his adoptive parents, his sister and his two little nephews at White House Farm in a blood-chilling case which dominated the newspapers for months. Tolleshunt d'Arcy was also the home, incidentally, of the best-selling author of whodunits in the 1930s, Margery Allingham.

Again, one of the manors belonging to Coggeshall Abbey was the manor of Thorndon, later bought by Lord Petre of Ingatestone Hall and transformed into a great estate. In the grounds was a colossal mausoleum to house the remains of all the Barons Petre, including some who had had their heads chopped off in times of political awkwardness. Thorndon Park was broken up after the First World War and bought by Essex County Council in 1939 and 1951, but the mausoleum remained. Some years later a man made the hazardous journey down a flight of grim dark stone steps to the crypt, stole two Petre heads, took them back up with him, and then flung them at doorways in Chelmsford, one of which was the police station. The man pleaded guilty to a minor charge of damage. No motive was ever admitted.

Chelmsford has been smarting for months with the agony of a particularly brutal, unsolved murder. Martin Broom, a 27-year-old bachelor of enormous local popularity, was battered to death as he lay asleep in bed at Sussex Close, Boreham. There are no suspects, there is no ascertainable motive, there is no forensic evidence. Martin left the Riverside Leisure Centre in Chelmsford at 10.45 p.m. on Friday, 21 July 1989, and went home to the semi-detached house he shared with lodgers. He had recently set himself up in business selling fork-lift trucks and was a frequent visitor to London night clubs. Very handsome, like Jeremy Bamber he attracted both men and women, though there seems no reason to think him bisexual. He had many lady friends and was considered by many to be a womaniser. Perhaps the husband of one of his lovers was irritated by his ardent attentions; perhaps one of the girlfriends herself grew tired of his fickleness. No one yet knows. The police literally haven't got a clue, for the simple reason that the murderer left none. There was no sign of forced entry, which means the killer was either let in by Martin, who then inexplicably got back into bed or, more likely, had his or her own key. A key could have been borrowed and copied. There were no fingerprints and no murder weapon. Everyone who knew Martin Broom has been interviewed, at least everyone the police know he knew, and everyone agrees he was the nicest of men, an agreeable companion without enemies.

If and when Martin's killer is found, his or her trial will be heard at Chelmsford Crown Court, where Wilfred Bull, Jeremy Bamber and scores of others have waited to learn their fate. It is a court through which some interesting criminals have passed, pursued by some flamboyant advocates. It was here that Mick McElligott, a barrister who later became a stipendiary magistrate and died in a tragic accident, was famed for his outrageous line of questioning. On one celebrated occasion McElligott said to an alibi witness in court, "Tell me, when you're dead, who will be the biggest liar in Essex?" The bar is much more polite these days, and any advocate who sought to emulate the theatricality of McElligott would soon have his knuckles rapped.

There can hardly have been a more bizarre case of rape than Regina v. Collins in 1971. Stephen Collins was 19 years old and randy. It was a Saturday night in Colchester, he had been drinking, and was keen to find a girl. He passed a house at three in the morning, where he spied a light on in a bedroom upstairs and the window open. He vaguely knew a girl who lived there with her mother, though not to speak to. She was 18. Collins found a step-ladder, placed it against the wall, and climbed up to the bedroom window. Peering in, he saw the girl lying asleep on top of the bed, a few inches away from the window; as the judge put it, "she has the habit of sleeping without wearing night apparel". Collins could hardly believe his luck. He descended the ladder and stripped off all his clothes except for his socks, then went back up again and pulled himself on to the window-sill, at which point the naked sleeper awoke, knelt on the bed, placed her arms around his neck and body and pulled him on top of her. They kissed and cuddled for about fifteen minutes. "I was rather dazed," said Collins, "because I didn't think she would want to know me."

But how wrong he was! The girl was under the impression throughout that her lover was indeed her lover, that is, her boyfriend, though she was not asked whether he generally effected his entry to her house through a first-floor window. After a while, she noticed certain things were wrong: the length of his hair, his voice as he muttered lust in her ear, and so on. She turned on the bedside light, discovered a stranger and ran to the bathroom. Stephen Collins then disappeared whence he had come, via the ladder. He was arrested the next day, tried, found guilty of burglary with intention to commit rape under the Theft Act of 1968, and sent to prison for 21 months. There was no dispute that sexual congress had taken place with consent. The girl contended that she would not have consented if she had known he was not her boyfriend, while Collins contended that he would not have proceeded had he not been so eagerly invited.

Collins's appeal was heard by Lord Justice Edmund Davies, whose summary of the facts deserves to be learnt by heart. In the course of his narration he described the girl's perceptions when she woke up and saw something on the window-ledge. "The young lady then realised several things: first of all that the form in the window was that of a male; secondly that he was a naked male; and thirdly that he was a naked male with an erect penis." She saw in the moonlight that his hair was blond, as was her boyfriend's, and leapt to the conclusion that he was paying her an ardent visit, although they had already been out together that evening.

The appeal rested on Stephen Collins's position on the window-sill at the moment the girl invited him to join her. If he was on the inside, he had then already entered the room and was guilty of trespass with intent to commit rape; but if he was on the outside sill, his entry was entirely by invitation and he was guilty of nothing criminal (indeed, he ought to have been congratulated for his intrepidity). Lord Justice Davies declared for the second interpretation of events and Collins was duly released from custody.

Essex, of course, also specialises as a refuge for crooks from London's East End; indeed, the two areas overlap, parts of Essex now falling into the metropolitan net. This circumstance accounts for much of the routine crime which keeps Chelmsford Crown Court ticking over nicely, if that is not too ironic an adverb. Added to which, the proximity of Tilbury Docks and Southend means that Essex is a splendid haunt of smugglers. Chelmsford hears about one case a week involving the smuggling of drugs and/or the concealment of smugglers, and many of these pull in the same old hands well known to police in the East End.

The police have had their troubles. Being so close to the wicked underworld of London brings unsavoury characters on to their patch, and there have been times when police officers have despaired of what they consider to be the "wetness" of judges. There was one such, legendary in parts of Essex, who was chairman of the Quarter Sessions, and had to deal with the administration of justice in the petty sessional division. He was called Thorpe, and he was notoriously hard of hearing. A barrister said of his court that "in no part of the country is justice administered with greater impartiality, for the chairman is stone deaf and hears not a word of evidence on either side".

Nevertheless, the criminal statistics are normal, until one gets close to Coggeshall. The frankly astonishing bundle of murders and suicides there since 1983 may also appear to be rooted in the usual motives – lust, jealousy, inadequacy and greed, essentially the same human failings as occur in any other country. But there is, just possibly, something different about these Coggeshall affairs, for they all suggest under scrutiny a common link, and that is a profound and abrupt change in personality.

The first of the Coggeshall murder mysteries surrounds the character of Diane Jones. She had been a social worker at the town hall in Braintree; reliable, steady, efficient, indeed one of the best they had ever employed, according to her superiors. She met Dr Jones of Lees Farm, Coggeshall and became his wife. Thereafter her behaviour disintegrated rapidly. She drank excessively, often to the point of distress in public, and indulged in promiscuous relationships with other men. Dr and Mrs Jones had a baby daughter, who was placed in care because the mother's drinking habits made her emotionally unstable – she had appeared in court on a drink-driving charge as well. As for the sexual adventures, she was said to flag down cars, lorries and motorbikes and then offer herself to the driver; following her disappearance, police interviewed at least 20 of her lovers in and around Coggeshall. She complained to neighbours that her husband beat her and that she was frightened of him and, according to one report, Diane said Dr Jones had threatened to kill her.

Whatever the case, the marriage was not a success. After only 11 months Diane was planning to seek a divorce, despite expecting another baby, and discussed the matter with a solicitor on Friday, 22 July 1983. The next afternoon she went to have her hair done. She was already drunk and causing some concern. Dr Jones came to collect her from the hairdressers and took her back to Lees Farm for a simple meal. But Diane was not satisfied that the day was at an end, so she asked her husband to take her to the Woolpack Inn, only half a mile from the farm. They arrived at 10.30 p.m. and had a drink. Diane became obstreperous, demanding they stay longer. A quarrel ensued, which only finished when Jones carried his protesting wife out in a fireman's lift. They drove home. Dr Jones parked the car, Diane waited at the front door, but when he walked round to join her she had disappeared. Jones never saw her again. He did not report her flight, as he was used to her going away without notice, then turning up just as suddenly a few days later. Nine days after her disappearance, however, he sold the Peugeot car in which she had taken her last journey. People in Coggeshall found it distinctly odd that Jones should have dealt with his priorities in such an unexpected order.

Diane Jones was ill-prepared for any kind of travel when she disappeared. She wore a simple mauve dress, and carried no handbag or money. The police searched Lees Farm on four separate occasions, looking under floorboards and even going so far as to rip up a new stretch of road just outside the house, which had been completed during the nine days which separated Diane's mysterious departure from her husband's decision to tell the world she was missing. Jones said he thought they were mad; he also knew he was their prime suspect.

His wife's body was found three months later, 34 miles away at Brightswell in Suffolk. She still wore the same dress, but her face had been so badly battered by what seemed to be a clawed hammer that it took several days before forensic scientists could positively identify her. The police were outraged by the brutality of Diane's end, their determination to find her killer intensified by pity for her suffering. Not only that, but they cursed the knowledge that the killer stood a very good chance of getting away with it, as the postulated hammer could not be found anywhere. "You can take it from me," said one officer, "this matter will not be left to rest. No one deserves to die like Diane Jones, no matter how she lived."

Jones was arrested and questioned for 55 hours. The file on Diane Jones was sent to the Director of Public Prosecutions, who advised that there was insufficient evidence to bring a case against her husband. He was released and returned to Lees Farm. The press continued to be fascinated by him, zooming in on his subsequent affairs with other women, most recently his fourth marriage, but the village folk, some of whom treat him with respect while others declare they would never trust him, could not forget the tragic descent of Diane Jones into a Dantesque existence of sex and alcohol. Dr Jones's friends hold the view that she was well on the road to ruin before her marriage; his detractors suggest that it could have been his drinking habits which influenced her. Either way, tests showed that she died within a few hours of leaving the Woolpack Inn on the night of 23 July.

Just down the road in West Street is Highfields Farm, which was the home of the millionaire antiques dealer Wilfred Bull and his bubbly wife Patsy. Theirs had been a splendidly successful marriage for 27 years – he the shrewd and careful businessman, she the bestower of social graces. Wilfred's parents had been in the antiques trade, so he knew the business as a professional, not as a dilettante who thinks selling old furniture might be a pleasant way to spend one's retirement. His knowledge of ivory carvings was serious and solid. Patsy was a warm and friendly soul, wonderfully at ease in company, cheerful, and in the habit of calling people "love" or "poor lamb". It was she who made their social life swing; their friends included Graham Hill, Harold Wilson and Princess Margaret. Wilfred suffered from a rare strain of leukaemia which at one point threatened to take his life within five years. He was horribly pessimistic and downcast and might well have given in had it not been for Patsy. It was she who insisted he should continue looking for a cure, consulting every expert in the field, trying every new drug, whether or not its efficacy had been demonstrated. As a result of this blitz, they eventually found a cure. Everyone said it was Patsy who had saved Wilfred's life.

Wilfred had not by any means been a faithful husband; Patsy knew of his affairs and accepted that he was an incorrigible womaniser. No lasting damage seemed likely until Wilfred began to see a great deal of another woman, who lived in Braintree. She was not discreet. She flaunted her relationship with Wilfred, turning up at awkward moments, waving and humiliating Patsy in public. Patsy went to see her to thrash it out, but they only succeeded in thrashing each other – Patsy leaving with a handful of the mistress's hair and a couple of bruises. It was after this that Patsy told Wilfred she wanted to discuss divorce.

He was 50 by this time, in May 1985, and she was 48. He might well have protected his marriage, as he had done in the past, by keeping his mistress in the half-light, rarely acknowledged. Or he might well have agreed to a divorce, which would not have harmed him financially; he was extremely rich, and his son was running the business in such a way as to make him even richer. Instead, he took his wife to their antiques warehouse a couple of hundred yards from the house and shot her in the brain with a pistol bullet. He then took the gun back to the house and placed it under the floor, together with some money taken from the safe. He was arrested the following day, charged with murder, tried and sentenced to life imprisonment. All for greed: it appeared that he could not face sharing his money with an ex-wife, so he killed her rather than give her a divorce settlement. It subsequently transpired that some 30 years earlier Wilfred had accidentally shot dead his 18-year-old brother with a shotgun as they jumped a ditch.

Barely a year after the tragedy of Patsy Bull another calamity befell yet another house in Coggeshall, Bouchiers Grange. This was the home of a stormy temperamental farmer called Jimmy Bell. He, too, had been married 27 years, and had two adult children. Rumour had reached Jimmy's ear that his wife Janet had been the top prize at a United States airbase in the county. The story was that the airmen played cards for her, and the winner then had sex with her in the lavatory. One cannot be surprised that Jimmy should be made angry by such an event; he felt that Janet had not merely betrayed but insulted him, and did not wait to enquire how much truth the rumour held. He placed a lavatory seat round his wife's neck and made her run the gauntlet at the airbase. Jimmy was charged with assault and sentenced at Chelmsford Crown Court to six months. Janet then divorced him.

Jimmy spent only five weeks of his sentence in gaol before he was released by the Court of Appeal, where presumably the account of Janet's behaviour was believed *in toto*. While awaiting trial he had met an exceedingly pretty girl called Augusta. She was only 18 and he was getting on for 50, but she loved him dearly, and Jimmy enjoyed all the bliss of renewal, the unparalleled masculine delight of a middle-aged youngster. Augusta was waiting for him when he came out of prison in 1982, and they were married shortly afterwards.

Their union was blessed with a daughter, Victoria, and their work for the local church made them especially popular with the old, who would be invited round to the Grange for tea. Jimmy's jealousy, however, grew, even though he had no grounds for his suspicions. Like Leontes in *The Winter's Tale*, he was convinced that, because he loved Augusta, so did everyone else, and in any competition for her affections he would be bound to lose. Their life together quickly became intolerable to her, fraught as it was by the continuous threat of argument and conflict. In 1986 she left him, taking the infant Victoria with her to her mother's house in Diss. At the beginning of June, Augusta secured an injunction restraining her husband from going near her mother's house, and an order denying him access to their child.

Jimmy was beside himself. Still deeply in love with Augusta, with a love rendered more powerful and exclusive by virtue of its being under threat, he could not bear her departure and openly advertised that he would kill Augusta and himself rather than face life without her. Nobody took the threats of murder seriously, although his sons did take the precaution of removing his collection of shotguns from the house.

But they left one behind. On 18 July he took a 12-bore shotgun with him to Diss, parked the car 500 yards from his mother-in-law's house, and walked down the road. Jimmy entered the house by the kitchen, where he saw his mother-in-law. Augusta was upstairs in the bathroom. As soon as she realised who was there, she telephoned her solicitor from the bedroom upstairs, then ran down in her bathrobe and fought with Jimmy. She managed to knock him over, which gave her mother the chance to make a dash for the door and escape with the baby. Augusta then screamed out from the window, "For God's sake help me, he's going to kill me!" And then he did, as she cowered in the corner, with a shot through her lungs. Augusta died within three minutes. Jimmy turned the shotgun on himself and blasted into his chest. He died instantly.

Back in Coggeshall three letters addressed to family and friends were found in the desk drawer. They had been written a full week earlier and they apologised for the murder and suicide in advance. He must have brooded on his nefarious intentions for long miserable hours alone. Coggeshall, when it doesn't change a personality, can make it sweat.

There were many who prayed that Peter Langan's personality might change – for the better. Though famous for his restaurants in London and Los Angeles, and locally known for the one in Stoneham Street, Coggeshall, he was often drunk or maudlin. Stories eddied around him; it was said that, when a customer complained about a cockroach on the floor, Langan ate it. His partner Michael Caine said of him, "Langan stumbles around in a cloud of his own vomit and is a complete social embarrassment. His mind is completely addled by booze." Not so addled that he could not rise to a riposte of some style. "Caine," he said, "is a mediocrity with halitosis, a man with a council house mind."

Langan had been married for 17 years. In 1989 his wife Susan asked for a divorce. Langan suggested they go out to dinner and go home for one last night together. Susan agreed. When they arrived at the house, Susan undressed and waited in the bedroom, but what she next saw was not a lamenting lover but a raging maniac. Langan poured petrol over himself and lurched in, brandishing matches. He set fire to himself, collapsed on to the wardrobe, fell on the bed, and set the house on fire. Susan escaped through a window. As he was carried out, Peter Langan said, "I did it, I want to die," and to his wife, "Susan, it was meant for me." He survived some seven weeks on a life-support system before finally succumbing to burnt flesh and scorched lungs. At the inquest, his wife said, "He was self-dramatising to a degree. He was rather given to trying to make his fancies real . . . something to show me despair and feelings of misery. I think he just lost control and wanted to make a grand gesture."

Lost control? What is it about Coggeshall that makes people go berserk? The terrible events at Tolleshunt d'Arcy a few miles away, when the Bamber family all perished at the hands of the handsome son Jeremy, testify to the opposite. Jeremy Bamber was so much in control, and so coldly, that before confessing to his girlfriend he planned the murders, carried them through in such a way as to make his dead sister appear the criminal, and even wept at their funerals. So convincing was he that the police did not suspect him until his uncle showed them some clues (rather too many for their comfort) which they had missed. At his trial much was made of his ability of strangle rats with his own hands; the fact that they had found his home-grown cannabis and were too stoned to resist does not detract from the awfulness of the image. Someone in court said Bamber was the most evil man he had ever set eyes upon. As an adopted son, no one was sure where Bamber had come from originally, at least until his trial set the hounds sniffing away. The mother and father he so mercilessly slaughtered were deeply religious, to the point where Bible readings and admonitions from God were a daily occurrence. Perhaps Jeremy was poisoned by religion. If so, it would not have been the first time in Essex.

In 1655 an 18-year-old Quaker called James Parnel burst into the church at Coggeshall and loudly charged the priest with blasphemy. He thereupon delivered his own address before being carted off in chains to Chelmsford Assizes.

Fined £40 and sent to prison until payment, Parnel was apparently cruelly treated in prison and died there 11 months later. It was said he starved himself to death for his faith.

In the years preceding this event, the whole of Essex had been held to ransom by a fanatically convinced witch-hunter called Matthew Hopkins. He began his professional career as a lawyer in Manningtree, Essex but when, in 1644, he spotted some witches living near him who met every six weeks on Friday and offered sacrifices to the Devil, he knew his vocation would be to exterminate them. Hopkins set himself up as a witch-hunter, roaming Essex in search of evil, unaware that he carried it within himself. If women could not recite the Lord's Prayer, or could walk backwards against the sun, or would not shed tears, Hopkins adjudged them to be the devils' children. They were weighed against the Bible, then thrown into a pool with thumbs and toes bound together. If they drowned they were innocent, if they survived, the hidden third nipple had saved them, so they were hanged. With such methods did Hopkins terrorise Essex for a number of years, until he was subjected to his own treatment and, not drowning, was hanged.

One other curiosity is deserving of a little attention. Some 50 years ago Alfred Watkins overhauled our understanding of prehistory with his seminal work on ley-lines. Tracking the incidence of mounds, moats and mark-stones across the entire country, he revealed that they were sophisticated tracks delineating lines of communication and direction arranged by our ancestors many centuries ago. The ley-lines, which may still be discerned by the attentive observer of topography, date in some cases from 4,000 BC and thus are the marks of a people whose religious or spiritual ideas were selected from our own. The point at which ley-lines crossed was a site of especially intense spiritual activity, and to this day many of our Christian churches stand on earlier sites which were selected for their spiritual qualities. Stonehenge is at one such junction. A

Chelmsford man in 1925 wrote of Essex that, "This is a country with very ancient earthworks, innumerable moats, mark-stones, stocks, mounds, camps etc . . . practically all the Essex churches lie in absolutely straight lines with outstanding sighting points at each end of the line; and almost every suggestive name such as Merk-stones, Mark's Ley, Stock, Cross Leys, etc. lies along these lines."

Coggeshall, where all these weird events have taken place, lies precisely at the junction of two such lines.

Harpers and Queen, March 1990

Genetic Fingerprinting

The Blooding by Joseph Wambaugh

In 1984 Alec Jeffreys discovered what is now known as genetic fingerprinting, the individually specific DNA map which each of us carries and which distinguishes us from everyone who is, ever was, or ever will be. Three years later, its usefulness was demonstrated in the most dramatic way, when it conclusively proved the innocence of one man and the guilt of another in a previously insolvable double murder case.

Lynda Mann, aged 15, was raped and strangled on a footpath in the village of Narborough, on the outskirts of Leicester, in 1983. The only clue was some semen, all other leads proving to be false.

Police almost despaired of finding the killer until another teenager, Dawn Ashworth, was murdered in similar style a mile or so away. Again, clues were scarce and unhelpful, but the police were convinced they had found their man when they arrested a kitchen porter who confessed, with some contradictory detail, to one of the crimes.

As the confession alone was legally unreliable, recourse was made to genetic fingerprinting to clinch the identification. It did nothing of the sort. The kitchen porter's blood showed not only that he was innocent but that one person (whose semen likewise carried his unique DNA map) was guilty of both of the killings.

Thus the porter became the first accused person in the world to be released as a result of the revolutionary technique. Heaven knows what would have happened to him without it. The murderer was eventually revealed when he tried to avoid the mass blood sampling in Narborough and surrounding villages.

Joseph Wambaugh tells the story with verve and skill, keeping us in the dark until he decides we should be progressively enlightened.

His advantage is that, having worked with the Los Angeles Police Department, he can avoid that shiver of prurience with which most true crime writers infect their descriptions of desecrated bodies.

He is also a sensitive man, who understands the unimaginable distress suffered by the parents of a murdered child, the "chaos, caprice and discontinuity" inflicted on their world.

On the other hand, he seems to have a beady eye on casting as he writes, so we have too much personal nonsense about the police officers and too many accounts of what the dramatis personae were wearing. Pity, because this is a serious subject which could benefit from a more academic approach.

Evening Standard, 26 January 1989.

Leopold and Loeb

On 21 May 1924, 13-year-old Bobby Franks did not come home from school after class finished at five o'clock. It normally took him a few minutes to walk the four blocks from Harvard School for Boys to the family home in Kenwood, a suburb of Chicago. His father, a wealthy and well-known businessman called Jacob Franks, searched the school and neighbouring streets for several hours, and was about to notify the police when he received a telephone call. The voice at the other end told him that Bobby had been kidnapped, was safe and well, and would be returned to his family on payment of $10,000 ransom. Should Franks refuse, or tell the police, Bobby would be killed.

By the nine o'clock post the following morning the distraught father received a typewritten note on plain white paper instructing him in what denomination to secure the money, and how to present it – in a small cigar-box wrapped in paper and sealed with wax. He was to sit by the telephone after 1 p.m. to await further directions.

At 12 noon the police called to tell Mr Franks that the body of a young boy had been found wedged in a concrete drain-pipe on a remote bank by the railway track. At 3 p.m. the telephone rang again. It was the kidnapper, informing him that a taxi would shortly arrive to take him to a drugstore. Franks scarcely knew what to believe. The taxi came and Franks was about to get in it, with the ransom money, when the telephone rang again. This time it was his brother-in-law with ghastly information; he had identified the body in the drain-pipe as that of young Bobby. The boy had been brutally murdered with repeated blows to the head.

There followed the most intensive manhunt in Chicago's criminal history. The newspapers went hysterical, and the police mercilessly grilled the most respectable schoolteachers in the hope of proving one a pervert. The taxi-driver who had been to collect Jacob Franks was cleared – he had simply been hired by telephone and went to the address as instructed. A man revealed that he had retrieved a bloodstained taped chisel which he had seen thrown from a car. Then came what looked like a more significant clue. A labourer working near the spot where the body had been found picked up from the ground a pair of horn-rimmed spectacles.

The spectacles were very ordinary and the prescription for the lenses extremely common. But one small detail was to prove crucial. The hinge on the glasses was a patented article, made by only one manufacturer in the United States, and this manufacturer used only one retail outlet in Chicago – Almer Coe and Company. Furthermore, Almer Coe had only been handling this frame with this particular hinge for a few months and their records showed they had sold a total of three pairs containing that prescription for lenses. One was to a lawyer, who had been in Europe for the past six weeks. A second to a lady, who still wore them. And the third to a young man called Nathan Leopold Jnr., who lived at 4754 Greenwood Avenue, very close both to the Harvard School for Boys and to the home of Bobby Franks.

The typewriter which had been used to prepare the ransom note was meanwhile recovered from the bottom of a lagoon in Jackson Park. At the same time, an enthusiastic boy named Richard Loeb, a fan of detective fiction, his pockets stuffed with newspaper accounts of the Franks killing, volunteered to help a newspaper reporter, telling him that the ransom call was probably made from a drugstore on 63rd Street and escorting him through the drugstores in the hope of tracking down the kidnapper.

Nathan Leopold was 19 years old, the son of a hugely wealthy millionaire from among the best-known families of Chicago. Known as "Babe" because he was the youngest, Leopold was extraordinarily intelligent and bright, with a Bachelor of Philosophy degree from the University of Chicago already, and currently studying law at the Chicago Law School. He was deemed by his contemporaries as something of a genius, for whom no subject was too abstruse, nor any reading too tedious. He had made a special study of works by the German philosopher Nietzsche. With money, brains and position, "Babe" was destined for a glamorous future, probably in public life. But the horn-rimmed glasses found by the body of Bobby Franks were his.

He did not deny ownership. When Leopold was picked up by two detectives and taken to be questioned by the State's Attorney, Mr Crowe, his family were having a big formal dinner party to celebrate the engagement of his older brother Mike. He was self-assured and unperturbed. Yes, he had a pair of horn-rimmed glasses, but he only wore them for bird-watching and had not had cause to use them lately. They were probably in an old suit at home which he kept for his bird-watching outings. The detectives drove him home again to look for them. They could not be found. Well, that's not so surprising, said Leopold. The railway bank where poor Bobby Franks's body was discovered (yes, he knew him!) was a well-known haunt of bird-watchers and Leopold had often been there. In fact, he taught ornithology and had taken his class there more than once. No doubt the glasses had fallen out of his pocket on one such occasion weeks ago.

The detectives persisted. Which pocket did he keep them in? The breast pocket. How could they have fallen out, did he think? He must have tripped. Show us, they said. Leopold tripped and tripped on the floor in front of the lawyers and detectives, but the glasses, placed by him in his breast pocket, stubbornly refused to be dislodged. Again and again he tried, succeeding only in making himself look foolish and the lawyers, for the first time, think that perhaps this golden boy could indeed be the man they were looking for. They intensified the questioning, going over the same points remorselessly, for hours on end. Leopold grew restive. How could they suspect him? Bobby Franks was a nice little boy, he said. The idea of ransom was absurd. He could have whatever money he wanted whenever he wanted, simply by asking his father; besides, he was paid for giving lessons in ornithology. All this could be easily corroborated (and was). He did not own an Underwood typewriter; his was a Corona.

Mr Crowe and his assistants then asked Leopold where he was on 21 May. By this time a week had passed and the young man could legitimately claim he could not remember precisely. But then he did. Yes, that was the day he had taken his own car out of the garage and gone to pick up a girl at Lincoln Park. Whom did he meet? What was her name? Whom was he with? Eventually, reluctantly, Leopold gave the name of his companion, an 18-year-old named Richard Loeb, the very one who was busy helping reporters solve the murder. He had not mentioned him before because the girls they had been with were not very respectable. They had both returned home late after their little adventure. Loeb was also rich and also a brilliant scholar. His father was the retired vice-president of the huge mail-order business, Sears, Roebuck and Co., and young Loeb was the youngest-ever graduate of the University of Michigan, a prodigy in fact. He had $3,000 of his own in the bank, and his father's secretary had instructions to make out any additional cheque for him at any time.

The Leopold's chauffeur, Sven, was called in. He had been with the family for nearly 19 years, since Nathan Leopold was a few months old. He would tell the truth and be sure to get Master Babe out of this mess. There was one day last week, he said, that Nathan did not take his car out of the garage. He remembered it precisely because it was the day his wife, Alma, had earache and had to go to the doctor. She had been prescribed some pills, and he still had the prescription written with the date on it – Wednesday 21 May. So Leopold's alibi was blasted; he had not been in his car with Dickie Loeb in Lincoln Park; he had not been in his car at all, for it had remained in the garage.

By this point Attorney Crowe was past being patient and polite. He told Leopold bluntly that his men were there and then taking a statement of confession from Richard Loeb at a police station seven miles away. He no longer needed Leopold to tell the truth – he already had it. Following the relentless questioning, this news drained Leopold of all resolve. He, too, confessed that he and Loeb had killed Bobby Franks, though it had been Loeb who actually struck the blow. The two boys were brought together before a panel of psychiatrists and made to tell their stories in the presence of each. Leopold was given pen and paper so he could make notes if Loeb tripped or got something wrong. The notes were later taken by Mr Crowe, who thereby had written as well as oral confessions to the crime.

The stories told by these two smart, clever, sophisticated boys revealed an account of a killing so pointless as to be without parallel in the history of murder.

Leopold and Loeb had been friends for a number of years. They were allied by intelligence and by emotion. Dickie Loeb was so enraptured by detective fiction that he would "shadow" people on the street to see if he could do it without being noticed, as if training himself for life as a professional sleuth. This reading was naturally additional to college books, which he could sail through with little effort, and also naturally secret. His governess had never approved of this interest, and so he had concealed it until it festered into fantasy. He determined that the perfect crime was possible given perfect preparation by a clever brain, and he thought he was capable of this perfect crime. Yet he needed an accomplice.

Nathan Leopold suited the bill admirably. His studies of Nietzsche had revealed to him the postulated "superman" who must be above considerations of morality, who had his own private code of right and wrong which was superior to ordained, shared codes, and which consisted baldly in the notion that whatever added to the experience of the individual and helped fulfil his potential as a personality was "right". It followed that whatever threatened to act against such personal fulfilment or experience was "wrong". Leopold was as enamoured of this philosophy as Loeb was of his crime novels. The combination was lethal.

In addition to which, Leopold was not a little in love with his friend. To him, Dickie Loeb was charm itself, an astonishing amalgam of good nature and easy companionship, of sharp mind and startling conversation, of loyalty and beauty. Leopold was captivated by Loeb and would do anything for him. The younger boy played on the older one's adoration. He would allow some sexual enjoyment on a regular basis if Leopold would join him in planning his perfect crime. Thus was the compact made.

Plans had been laid months before. The boys opened separate bank accounts under assumed names, and Leopold established credit under the false name with a rent-a-car firm. This would be the one they would use for the crime, to abduct a rich boy, kill him, and extract ransom money from his family before his death became known. They also registered in hotels, using the pseudonyms to create an identity and history for these invented people. They agreed they would kill by strangulation, thus sharing the responsibility (this part of the plan was not adhered to), and they agreed where to conceal the body so that it would not be found for a long time (this part went immediately wrong).

The victim's father would be brought to the drugstore on 63rd Street, where he would receive another telephone message instructing him to board a train and look for a piece of paper in the rack at a place to be specified. The paper would tell him to hurl the cigar-box containing the $10,000 from the moving train at a precise location, where one of the two would be waiting to retrieve it. There seemed no way in which the crime could be traced to either of them.

Some time before April they stole an Underwood typewriter from Ann Arbor, the town in Illinois where the university resides. On 20 May they composed the ransom note together, Leopold doing the typing on paper bought especially for the purpose. The next day they went looking for their victim, in the car hired under the false name. The first boy they saw was Bobby Franks. He was chosen at random. Bobby knew both Nathan and Dickie and did not hesitate, therefore, to get into the car when they offered to show him a new tennis racket. Leopold was driving. Bobby got into the back seat with Dickie Loeb, who almost immediately hit him over the head with a taped chisel several times, and stuffed a cloth soaked with hydrochloric acid into his mouth. The little boy was soon unconscious and bled profusely. Loeb covered him with a rug. It became saturated with blood which flowed on to the floor of the car.

Leopold drove to the edge of Chicago into open country and stopped. Bobby's shoes were removed and hidden in some bushes by the road. They unbuckled his belt and took off his trousers and socks, throwing the belt into the street but leaving the clothes in the car. Then, incredibly, they went to a roadside café and left the now dead boy's body in the car while they went in to eat some sandwiches. The nonchalance is astonishing but not isolated. After picking up Bobby Franks they had driven past their own and his houses, and might easily have been seen by neighbours who knew all three of them! Having eaten, they returned to the car with its pitiful occupant and set about disposing of the body.

The part of the railroad track between 118th and 123rd Streets, where Leopold had indulged his bird-watching, was swampy and quiet. Here they stripped the remainder of Bobby's clothes and jammed his naked body, head first, into the concrete pipe. Leopold waded into the swamp in boots to hide some of the boy's bloodstained clothes in mud, then returned to the car and put on his shoes. About nine o'clock in the evening they began to head back to their homes; at this time, Jacob Franks was still tramping the streets in search of his son. Leopold stopped at a drugstore to call home and warn that he would be late. They threw the chisel out of the window and went on to Loeb's home where they lit a fire in the basement and burned what was left of Bobby Franks's clothes. They washed the rug of blood and tried to clean the floor of the hired car. Then Leopold made the first telephone call to Mr Franks demanding the ransom, and posted the letter which would arrive the following morning at a mailbox in Hyde Park Boulevard. Loeb was with him in both transactions.

The two left the car in a street nearby and went to Leopold's home at 10.30 p.m., where they played cards until midnight, and Leopold drove Loeb home in his own car. The next morning they abandoned the rented car in another street and Loeb bought his ticket for the train wherein he placed the note destined to be found, according to the plan, by Mr Franks from a drugstore and sent the taxi on its errand to collect the unfortunate man. But as he left the drugstore he saw the newspaper headlines announcing that Bobby Franks's body had already been found. He thereupon returned the rented car and went home, where Sven, the chauffeur, told him the news of the murder.

The next day, 23 May, Leopold and Loeb both drove to the Jackson Park Lagoon and twisted off the keys of the typewriter which they threw into the water, together with the remains of the typewriter. They soaked the rug in petrol and burned it. They knew by then that the ransom would not be paid, but they had no need of the money anyway and were confident that every clue had been destroyed. Neither of them realised that the old bird-watching suit Nathan Leopold had elected to wear for the occasion contained a pair of spectacles which would inexorably direct investigators to one of them.

As it happened, the perfect crime proved to be the game of children, for once the confessions were checked every detail shouted its condemnation. Bank and hotel employees corroborated the aliases they had used; shops where they had bought the chisel, the paper, and the hydrochloric acid all produced employees who had clear memories of the various sales; a ticket salesman at the railway station identified Richard Loeb as the person to whom he sold a ticket for the Michigan train; the note was found on the train and the typewriter found in the lagoon. The case against Leopold and Loeb was complete, without a hole, with no possibility of retraction.

Until the revelation of the horn-rimmed spectacles a week later both boys had been remarkably cool and untroubled, even cold-hearted. They met for lunch. Dickie Loeb was elated, even whistling with excitement. Leopold attended dinner parties at home, sat for law exams and laid plans for a trip to Europe in the summer. He even read French poetry to a girlfriend, his head romantically on her lap.

On 11 June Nathan Leopold and Richard Loeb were indicted on two counts of murder and kidnapping. Initially they pleaded not guilty, but their powerful families secured the services of lawyers who were friends of the Loebs, the brothers Bachrach, and finally the greatest American defence lawyer of the century, Clarence Darrow. Darrow would both change the plea to guilty, and transform a squalid tale of premeditated murder into one of the most famous trials of all time.

On 21 July 1924, Leopold and Loeb appeared before Judge Caverly at Cook County Criminal Court, with Clarence Darrow defending, assisted by Benjamin and Walter Bachrach, and State's Attorney Robert Crowe prosecuting, assisted by Thomas Marshall and the aptly named Joe Savage. Mr Crowe had brought two separate indictments, for murder and kidnapping. If the verdict went against him on one indictment, he intended to spring the other and thereby oblige a second trial.

To avoid this, Mr Darrow unexpectedly, on behalf of his clients, pleaded guilty to both charges, a plea which was accepted before Crowe realised what was happening. Darrow said there was no dispute about the facts of the case, that he would offer no contention against any of the evidence assembled by Mr Crowe, and that he might as well get it all over with quickly. Darrow intended to present evidence in mitigation, appertaining to the state of mind of the defendants. Crowe objected that there could be no question of insanity on a guilty plea in Illinois; Darrow replied that he did not seek to show his clients were insane, only that their minds were diseased, and this for the court to consider when determining what punishment would be appropriate. In other words, Darrow would not suggest the boys were innocent, but he would pitch all his effort towards saving them, none the less, from the death sentence. There was more chance of this being achieved on a guilty plea before a judge, than on a not guilty plea which would be heard by a jury.

The trial opened on 23 July. It was to last three months, in a small, stifling courtroom crowded with journalists from all over the world and dominated by the stooping, shuffling and shabby figure of Clarence Darrow, in short-sleeves and braces, looking like an embarrassing senile relation. (He was 67 years old.) Attorney Crowe was not to be deprived of his opportunity to present the fullest possible case, despite the guilty plea, and called well over a hundred witnesses, only one of whom was cross-examined by Darrow.

Thomas Marshall had done his homework in the history books, and informed the court of all the precedents in the State of Illinois which demanded the death penalty, even for minors as Leopold and Loeb technically were, attempting to show that the judge would fulfil his duty only in putting these boys to death. Joe Savage vented the wrath of the common man upon the court, speaking of horror and disgust, dwelling on the suffering of little Bobby Franks and the heinous loathsome character of his murderers, crying out with passionate rage for justice to be done in the only manner acceptable, to rid the earth of such foul people.

("Did they choose him for his name?" wondered Darrow.)
"This is the coldest-blooded murder that the civilised world
ever saw," Savage said. "No one would strike a dog the way
these murderers had beat the life out of poor little Bobby
Franks with a cold chisel. If these two escape the gallows,
no jury in Cook County could thereafter be expected to
inflict upon any defendant, no matter how depraved, the
extreme penalty for murder and kidnapping."

When Darrow rose to present the case for the defence,
he began by disdainfully pitying the excessive anger of the
prosecutors. "It seems to me," he said, "if I could ever
bring my mind to ask for the death penalty, I would do
it not boastfully and exultantly or in anger or hate, but I
would do it with the deepest regret that it must be done,
and I would do it with sympathy even for the ones whose
lives were to be taken. That has not been done in this case.
I have never seen a more deliberate effort to turn the
human beings of a community into ravening wolves and
take advantage of everything that was offered to create an
unreasoned hatred against these two boys." The effect of
this speech, delivered slowly with grave deliberate pauses
and a low tremulous voice, was immediately to make the
prosecuting counsel appear too eager and somewhat less
honourable, while Darrow, for his part, would carry the
burden of the case with dignity, humanity and the deep
thought which such a case merited.

Darrow's witnesses were psychiatrists, or "alienists" to
give them the name by which such professional men were
then known. Leopold and Loeb had been examined by
no less than 14 doctors, and three of the most eminent
in America were called to give evidence. They were Dr
William White, the dean of all American psychiatrists and
head of the country's largest mental hospital; Dr William
Healy, acknowledged expert on juvenile psychopathy; and
Dr Bernard Glueck, the country's best-known authority
on criminal psychology. They examined the boys' history,

character and physical condition, and their testimony established at the very least an intellectual attachment between Leopold and Loeb which was intense and dangerous.

Richard Loeb had been in the hands of a rigid authoritarian governess from the age of 11, a woman who managed his life to the extent of deciding what friends he should be permitted and how he should spend his leisure hours. He escaped her influence by reading crime stories and by mixing with older boys. He was subject to frequent fainting fits, sometimes as many as six in a day, during which he would assume rigidity and froth at the mouth. He had contemplated suicide. He became deceitful and unscrupulous, and eventually determined he would assert his individuality by committing the perfect crime. Initially a fantasy, it became a fixation, and was so totally removed from normal moral considerations that he considered his own younger brother as a possible victim. His school-friends declared they found him childish, always ready to scare people for no reason or to laugh at misfortune. Darrow depicted him as an emotional cripple, a boy of 18 who remained stuck at a pre-pubescent stage of fantasy and hallucination.

Nathan Leopold was also brought up with nurses and governesses, and his father had unwittingly instilled in him the notion that because he was wealthy he was inherently superior to other boys. When he was 14 his governess seduced him into unusual sexual practices. Also by 14 he had taught himself to speak several languages fluently and showed an intellectual capacity far in excess of the norm. He was reading deeply into religion and philosophy, and by 16 had rejected all religions and declared himself an atheist. He adopted Nietzschean philosophy wholesale and openly stated that he was not subject to ordinary ethical considerations. Leopold was not a handsome boy – his large protruding eyes made him feel ugly and imperfect. Richard Loeb, on the other hand, was very good looking. Leopold fantasised about being slave to a superman whom he would idolise and to whom he could submit himself in obedience. He was 15 when he met Loeb and found his hero.

Letters which Leopold had written to Loeb indicated the degree of his infatuation, which was abject and ultimately demeaning. Their emotional content ran counter to Darrow's portrait of a boy who was pure mind, intellect without scruple, a boy whose emotional existence had been smothered by a combination of spoiling indulgence and unfettered mental development. By the time the alienists had finished, there stood before the court an image of a perverse accident, that these two, with their different failings and their privileged lives, met and fitted each other's needs like pieces of a jigsaw puzzle. Neither was finally responsible for his genes or the whimsy of fate which brought them together.

Psychiatrists called by the prosecution were given a hard time by Mr Darrow. They admitted they had spent very little time with the defendants. One of them had never met the boys, but based his evidence solely upon observations in court. Another suffered the embarrassment of having Darrow read out from his own books opinions which contradicted those he had expressed in court and showed that he in fact agreed with the defence analysis of the boys' characters. The chief expert for the prosecution was Dr Krohn, a man who had made his living in recent years precisely by appearing in court to give evidence in scores of cases. As far as he was concerned, Leopold and Loeb were the two sanest, healthiest individuals he had ever examined. They betrayed no conduct which could in any way be termed abnormal, save in their utter indifference to the enormity of their crime.

Darrow treated this man with such ferocious scorn it would appear he might never be asked to give evidence again. "I do not care what Dr Krohn may say," said Darrow with a dismissive wave of the hand. "He is liable to say anything, except to tell the truth, and he is not liable to do that . . . Krohn, who by his own admissions, for 16 years has not been a physician, but has used a licence for the sake of haunting these courts, civil and criminal, and going up and down the land peddling perjury."

With that, Clarence Darrow would have nothing more to do with the State's so-called experts. He ignored the rest of their testimony and saved his oratory for his final address to the court. This began on 22 August.

The atmosphere in court was electric when Darrow rose to make his speech. It was to go on for a total of 12 hours, and so dramatic was its delivery, so intense its feeling, that it appeared the old man was making the statement of his life, his last chance to plead not just for Leopold and Loeb but for the whole of suffering humanity. There was a feeling in court that he and he alone stood between these two young men and the braying mob which would tear them apart. "When the public speaks as one man," he said, "it thinks only of killing."

Clarence Darrow attacked the violence of the prosecution, examined the lack of motive for the murder, and dealt with the influence of Nietzschean philosophy, building his argument towards a moving personal exposition of his abhorrence of capital punishment. To the prosecutor he said, "You may stand them up on the trap-door of the scaffold, and choke them to death, but that act will be infinitely more cold-blooded, whether justified or not, than any act that these boys have committed or can commit. Let the State, who is so anxious to take these boys' lives, set an example in consideration, kind-heartedness and tenderness before they call my clients cold-blooded . . . This world has been one long slaughterhouse from the beginning until today, and killing goes on and on and on, and will for ever. Why not read something, why not study something, why not think instead of blindly shouting for death? . . . If the State in which I live is no kinder, more humane, more

considerate, more intelligent than the mad act of these two
boys, I am sorry that I have lived so long."

Darrow rehearsed the facts of the case from the point
of view of motive. There was none, he said. There was
no cause for revenge, no hatred, no need for money, no
explanation whatever. They killed Bobby Franks for the
experience, and if that does not demonstrate a diseased
mind, then nothing will. "You may search the annals of
crime, and you will find no parallel. It is utterly at variance
with every motive and every act and every part of conduct
that influences normal people in the commission of crime.
There is not a sane thing in all of this from the beginning
to the end. There was not a normal act in any of it, from
its inception in a diseased brain, until today, when they
sit here awaiting their doom."

Part of Darrow's technique was always to refer to the defendants as "boys", implying that they had not yet reached
the age of judgment or maturity. With the same purpose, he
referred to "Dickie Loeb" and "Babe Leopold" almost with
affection, as their parents would have done, thus removing
from them the stigma of monstrosity which anonymity
or naked surnames might bestow. Darrow had constantly
to remind the court that the defendants were as human
as their victim and their prosecutors. "From the age of 15
to the age of 20 or 21, the child has the burden of adolescence, of puberty and sex thrust upon him. Girls are
kept at home and carefully watched. Boys without instruction are left to work the period out for themselves.
It may lead to excess. It may lead to disgrace. It may
lead to perversion. Who is to blame? Who did it? Did
Dickie Loeb do it?" The court must resist the temptation
to make Loeb responsible for his personality and the perverse avenue it took simply in order to have a hanging.

Turning to Leopold, Clarence Darrow spoke at length
on the subject of literature and its ability to influence the
behaviour of a young impressionable mind. "Your Honour,

I have read almost everything that Nietzsche ever wrote. He was a man of wonderful intellect, the most original philosopher of the last century. A man who has probably had a deeper imprint on philosophy than any other man within a hundred years ... Nathan Leopold is not the only boy who has read Nietzsche. He may be the only one who was influenced in the way that he was influenced."

Religious fanatics may teeter on the edge of insanity by virtue of their extravagant beliefs; some end their lives in lunatic asylums. So it is with a fanatical adherence to a philosophy, which is not more nor less than an alternative religion. If the tenets of the philosophy are swallowed entirely, without scrutiny or criticism, they too may lead to madness. Nietzsche himself, said Darrow with tremendous effect, was insane for the last 15 years of his life. "His very doctrine is a species of insanity." Leopold became infected with this doctrine. It is there for all to see and read, in every library, in every university. Nietzsche is taught in our schools, discussed in our classes. There is no secret about it. "Your Honour, it is hardly fair to hang a 19-year-old boy for the philosophy that was taught at the university.

"A boy with a beautiful home, with automobiles, a graduate of college, going to Europe, and then to study law at Harvard; as brilliant in intellect as any boy that you could find; a boy with every prospect that life might hold out to him; and yet he goes and commits this weird, strange, wild, mad act, that he may die on the gallows or live in a prison cell until he dies of old age or disease ... Can Your Honour imagine a sane brain doing it? Can you imagine it coming from anything but a diseased mind?" Darrow drove very close to the legal notion of *res ipsa loquitur*, "the thing speaks for itself", the idea that the defendants must be crazy to have done what they did, or they would not have done it. It is a circular argument ruthlessly pounced upon by prosecutors, and one which Darrow was careful to avoid. But he managed to plant the seed without actually saying so.

He also managed to turn in the defendants' favour the prejudice which prevailed against their wealth. If they had not been so rich they would not have encountered such enmity from the public and the State's Attorney. "Great wealth often curses all who touch it."

After over 11 hours on his feet, Clarence Darrow approached the peroration of his address and of his career. He turned to what he called the "superstition" that hanging a man somehow stops another man from committing a crime. It was a superstition that men clung to with appalling tenacity. He spoke about the history of hanging as an exhibition and the squalor it heaped upon the souls of those who saw it. He reminded the court that civilisation had advanced and that no person under 23 had ever been hanged in Illinois on a plea of guilty. The defendants must not be at large, Darrow knew that; they must be kept from the public and deprived of all freedom. For their sake, it might be merciful to kill them, but not merciful to civilisation, and not merciful to those of us who are left behind. Not to the parents of both boys who, like the grieving Mr Franks, had looked forward to a splendid future for the sons upon whom they thought they had showered the best of all love.

Nathan Leopold tried, at this point, to prevent himself from crying, but without success. Richard Loeb, too, dug his fists into his eyes in a desperate bid for control, and portrayed a potent image of helpless childhood as susceptible to emotion, after all, as any ordinary person. Judge Caverly concentrated his attention upon Darrow, his chin resting in his hand, as if nothing but an earthquake would deflect him. The whole room was mesmerised by the power and passion of Darrow's Ciceronian prose, which proceeded as if isolated from time, against a background of absolute, uncanny silence. It was one of the rare occasions when an advocate is heard and heeded, and when he may move opinion.

"I wish to make no false pretence to this court. The easy thing and the popular thing to do is to hang my

clients. I know it. Men and women who do not think
will applaud. The cruel and thoughtless will approve. It will
be easy today; but in Chicago, and reaching out over the
length and breadth of the land, more and more fathers and
mothers, the humane, the kind and the hopeful, who are
gaining an understanding and asking questions not only
about these poor boys, but about their own – these will
join in no acclaim at the death of my clients . . . I know
Your Honour stands between the future and the past. I
know the future is with me, and what I stand for here; not
merely for the lives of these two unfortunate lads, but for all
boys and all girls; for all of the young and, as far as possible,
for all of the old. I am pleading for life, understanding,
charity, kindness, and the infinite mercy that considers all.
I am pleading that we overcome cruelty with kindness,
and hatred with love. I know the future is on my side."

The weary old man, who could hardly look forward to
much future for himself, used his plea on behalf of Leopold
and Loeb almost unconsciously as his personal testament
to the virtues and highest attributes of life. He hoped he
might have done something to temper justice with mercy,
and he finished with a quotation from Omar Khayyám,
then stood quietly for a moment before resuming his seat.
Two full minutes went by before anyone dared cough. One
reporter wrote, "There was scarcely any telling where his
voice had finished and where silence had begun. His own
eyes, dimmed by years of serving the accused, the op-
pressed, the weak, were not the only ones that held tears."

Indeed they were not. Not a breath of air moved in the
courtroom, but Judge Caverly sat with tears streaming
down his face.

Every newspaper in Chicago printed the whole of Clarence
Darrow's speech, as did many throughout the United States.
Never before had such a tribute been paid to a working
advocate. The speech was later published as a pamphlet

and quickly became a best-seller. But the trial was not over yet.

State's Attorney Crowe spoke for two days against Darrow's view of the case, with a maddened fury which no longer matched the public mood. He virtually shouted himself hoarse. Leopold and Loeb, he said, were ruthless killers "as little entitled to sympathy and mercy as a couple of rattlesnakes, flushed with venom, and ready to strike." Crowe airily dismissed all the nonsense about fantasies and literature and pacts, attempting to belittle Darrow for his naivety. The case was simple, he said. Leopold knew something about Loeb and blackmailed him into submission to his sexual desires. They both planned the murder with meticulous thoroughness, over several months, and they both executed it. Neither had shown any remorse. The motive was money – $10,000 to be precise – and to pretend otherwise was idiotic.

Crowe attacked the defendants' wealth, referring to Darrow as a "million-dollar defence" who had been bought by greed and venality. He also attacked Darrow's personal character. Over and over again he repeated that Darrow was "an atheist, the same as his clients". He was "the exponent of a philosophy as dangerous as Leopold's" and "a paid advocate whose profession it was to protect murder in Cook County, and concerning whose health thieves enquire before they go out to commit crime." It was a desperate performance by a man who was frustrated at having won the case but lost the argument.

Judge Caverly adjourned until 10 September, by which time he said he would have reached a decision. To avoid public demonstration or panic, he would bar the court to all but the defendants, their families and their counsel.

On 10 September 1924, after nearly three months of the strain attendant upon a trial so much in the public eye, the judge announced that it was his duty to explain the reasons for his decision in view of the world-wide interest which had been shown. There was no doubt of the defendants' guilt. He had listened to arguments presented in mitigation, but could find no grounds for supposing Leopold and Loeb were afflicted with any more abnormality than would be found in any criminal or murderer. He could not therefore allow any mitigating circumstances. Furthermore, while the issue of human responsibility for individual acts was of lasting interest to philosophers, it was of no consequence to the court, which was bound to enforce the law as it stood and not as it ought to stand or might stand in the future.

"The testimony in this case reveals a crime of singular atrocity," continued Judge Caverly. "It is in a sense inexplicable, but it is not thereby rendered less repulsive and inhumane. It was deliberately planned and prepared for during a considerable period of time. It was executed with every feature of callousness and cruelty." He made a particular point, missed by most newspapers, that there was no evidence the victim had been subjected to any sexual molestation whatever, but that did not make the crime any less revolting. There was, in short, nothing to alleviate the awfulness of what these two young men had done.

Prosecuting counsel looked understandably satisfied as the judgment proceeded, and the defendants correspondingly despondent. Caverly read the statutes and listed the punishments laid down. It would be easy to follow the line of least resistance and impose the extreme penalty of the law. But the alternative was open to him to send the defendants to prison for the rest of their lives, and he was inclined to that alternative in consideration of the age of the two boys and his reluctance to impose death upon men who had not reached full maturity. Such a sentence was in accordance with progress in criminal law all over the Western world and also with the thought of enlightened humanity.

The Court sentenced Nathan Leopold and Richard Loeb to life imprisonment on the count of murder, and to 99 years' imprisonment on the count of kidnapping.

Messrs Crowe, Marshall and Savage were completely stunned by this change of direction in the judge's remarks; they were confident of a death sentence until the very last seconds. The defendants, on the other hand, were not elated, but showed subdued relief. Leopold and Loeb were taken to the Joliet penitentiary and to the history books.

Marshall Cavendish.

Andrei Chikatilo

The market in books about so-called "serial" murders is already overloaded with shallow confections. However, Robert Cullens's *The Killer Department* (Orion £15.99), about the murders committed by Andrei Chikatilo in Russia over eight years, differs from most books in several respects. To start with, it describes the first time that the Russians admitted that a severe aberration of human behaviour was possible in the glorious perfection of communist society. Knife-wielding sexual perverts were supposed only to happen in a decadent bourgeois milieu, which meant that if they did turn up in Russia the public could not be informed. The Chikatilo case began under the Soviets and was solved after Gorbachev and *glasnost* had rendered concealment obsolete. It is the first such case to be thoroughly examined and reported.

Second, the detective in charge of the case had the courage to trust modern Western psyshiatric methods, which had been forbidden in Soviet Russia as pernicious, for they suggested that human frailty and misery had little to do with the absence of Marxist economic bliss. The author is right to tell this appalling story from the detective's point of view, enabling us to engage in two parallel experiences – the

tracking down of the murderer and the emergence of
Russian crime detection from a prolonged age of darkness.

From 1982 until 1990, a shocking sequence of murders baffled the police headquarters at Rostov-on-Don.
The victims ranged from pubescent girls or boys to mature
young women, but the brutality of their killer was constant. Bodies had been mutilated in such a way as to
indicate sexual obsession (removal of uterus or testicles),
and also a degree of cruelty scarcely imaginable. One nine-
year-old boy's neck was encircled with multiple shallow
knife wounds, indicating sadistic pleasure in their inflic-
tion while the boy was still alive.

There being no press reports in the early stages of the
investigation, rumours abounded. Five false confessions
were made and one man was actually imprisoned. Still the
murders went on, gathering in frequency and in the intensity
of savagery they manifested. Lieutenant Colonel Viktor
Burakov, placed in charge of finding the man, was determined to break all the rules, if necessary, to stop him. The
hunt became a personal quest for Burakov, poisoning his
nights as well as stretching his days, almost leading to what
we would term (although he did not) a nervous breakdown.

The Soviet psychiatrists came up with contradictory
ideas, and concluded that there were two murderers,
and that one of them was homosexual. This led to a
frenetic search in all the tightly closed closets of Rostov
and a superfluous and unnecessary purge. More than 100
homosexual men were imprisoned, and three committed
suicide rather than face public obloquy. Burakov then
made his most crucial decision. He called in a psychiatrist, Aleksandr Bukhanovsky, who was well versed
in Western understanding of personality disorders, and
turned over all the files to him. Bukhanovsky came up
with a "profile" of the likely killer which was astonishingly close to the man eventually arrested. But so
unconventional, in Soviet terms, was their approach to

the case that he and Burakov had to work almost in
secrecy.

A homosexual called Ivanenko was eliminated from the
enquiry, but he so impressed Burakov with his intelligence and intuition that he became another unofficial
member of the investigating team and the two men became
friends. A convicted murderer called Slivko, who was due
to be executed for the slaying of seven boys, was likewise
interviewed and consulted. The most illuminating insight
which he provided was that the man they were looking
for would most likely turn out, paradoxically, to be
significantly moral in his attitudes. Through all this, one
has the feeling that Burakov was prepared to educate
himself out of the restrictions of Soviet thinking, and if
he needed the assistance of an intellectual, a homosexual
and a convict in the process, then so be it.

When, after 56 murders, Chikatilo was eventually caught,
he was interrogated by the official doctor, a man whose
crass approach caused the suspect to sink deeper into sullen
shame and to refuse the exposure of a confession. Burakov
suggested Bukhanovsky be allowed to talk to him, a request
granted only on condition that Bukhanovsky should not
give evidence in any subsequent court. Within two hours
of their meeting, Chikatilo confessed; it was clear that his
shame, his rage and his history of humiliation needed to
be expressed, and he himself was bright enough to know
they also needed to be explained.

Chikatilo was a quiet, submissive man who played chess
with his son-in-law and who hankered after a decent library.
He was married with two children, had once applied to law
school in Moscow, was a party member and had also been
a teacher. An unremarkable man save that he had also
regularly bitten off the nipples off corpses and swallowed
them. The latter part of this book traces his descent from inadequacy into sadism with remorseless candour. Although
there are some passages of reflection, the tone is, frankly,

that of a chronicle. Cullen was Moscow's bureau chief for *Newsweek*, and his excellent reporting style is shorn of all decoration.

This style works best in Cullen's account of the ludicrous trial last year, in which the judge appeared to think he was locked in battle with the defendant. There is much which is bound to offend an American nurtured on the principle that you are not required to tell the truth if it goes against your interests, but Cullen is wrong to discern any fundamental difference between the Russian and Western approaches to the insanity defence. Such a defence was rejected in the case of Chikatilo, who was found guilty and now awaits execution, for precisely the same reasons as it habitually fails in Britain and America, namely that lawyers cannot see madness when it escapes their definitions; they will not allow that a sequence of sane, logical and premeditated acts might lead towards an insane, illogical and compulsive purpose. In their limited understanding, planning equals sanity, and they will resist all psychiatric attempts to have them think more deeply.

In his anxiety to show the superior humanity of the American system, Cullen makes a crucial and telling error. Jeffrey Dahmer, he says, was judged insane in Milwaukee. Well, he wasn't, and that is precisely the point. Cullen's book has the value, perhaps not intended, of demonstrating that in our appraisal of sanity, we are still no better than the Russians.

The Sunday Times, 9 May 1993.

CHAPTER 5

The Ethical Debate I

It has recently become more and more clear that public interest in murder, especially what I call addictive murder, is virtually insatiable. Paperback treatments of diverse killers could be published every week and still find an audience, and the appetite for explicit, harrowing films is growing exponentially. This phenomenon raises the perennial question as to how far the artist, be he writer or film director, should be held responsible for the moral content or influence of his work.

The obvious, easy answer is that he must not be accountable to moral authority in any circumstances. To suggest otherwise is to invite the old bogeyman of censorship, the enemy of artistic freedom. The artist is not a priest, but a chronicler and interpreter, who reflects through the prism of his understanding the knowledge he finds before him. If, therefore, a murderer has committed a number of heinous acts, it is his fault they are heinous, not the fault of the man who reports or relates them.

Ethical matters are never so simple, however. Some filmmakers are less interested in the truth of artistic endeavour than they are in providing commercially successful entertainment. There is nothing intrinsically terrible about commercial success, of course, but when it conflicts with moral responsibility we are entitled to ask which should take precedence. Does the film-maker owe any duty of truthfulness, probity, honesty to his audience? Or should

he simply give them what they want, even if that be un-
truthful, dishonest, unprincipled?

There are different ways in which films may let the
audience down. *Reversal of Fortune* appeared deliberately
to traduce the character of Claus von Bülow because his
innocence of the charges brought against him did not fit
the demands of entertainment. He needed to be a villain,
or the film would not have one, and would lack the necessary ingredient at the centre. This was an instance of a film
giving the wrong impression, manipulating the audience
into thinking that a man charged with attempted murder must be guilty of something, especially if he is so
smooth. In the first article reprinted in this chapter, I
went into the evidence set forth at the trial to show how
grievously immoral was this attitude.

In the second film review I discuss why *The Silence of the
Lambs* was reprehensible for quite other reasons. In the first
place, it invited the audience to look upon the murderer as
a man to be envied, admired, applauded for his cleverness.
The character of Hannibal Lecter almost seduced them
into complicity. Moral discomfort was suddenly irrelevant,
unfashionable. In the second place, the character was im-
plausible, as Dennis Nilsen himself pointed out, because
"serial" killers would not need to become killers if they
already had such powers of intellect and control as Lecter
appeared to possess. This film sacrificed everything to the
need to entertain, and was thereby fraudulent.

The third piece considers once more the distinction between entertainment and literature, or fun and catharsis,
prompted by a television programme about the murder of
Rachel McLean in Oxford 1991, and looks at the theme
which is a constant leitmotif of my writing on this subject, namely the dangers of infection by the subject itself.
Parenthetically, it is also a cause for worry that the Rachel
McLean case attracted the attention of newspaper editors
for reasons only tangential to the essence of the crime. Miss

McLean was young, she was pretty, she was intelligent, she would have made a lovely wife. At about the same time, the body of Jo Ramsden was discovered and reported, but she was given less coverage. Miss Ramsden was also young and much loved, but she was a Down's syndrome girl, and the inadmissible inference from her comparative neglect by the press was that such a girl might be considered, from an *audience* point of view, as less of a "star" victim than an Oxford undergraduate. In such subtle ways are our ethical responses occasionally manipulated.

The last film review covers *The Krays*, and happily celebrates the moral value to which a serious film may attain. It went so far as to demolish, for a while at least, my liberal predilections, which entirely disappeared when I saw just how loathsome were the notorious twins. *The Krays* is violent, certainly – and in some scenes as violent as the lamentable *Henry: Portrait of a Serial Killer* – but its purpose is, on balance, not merely to titillate or entertain, but to offer an honest portrayal of a difficult subject. The purpose, in ethical matters, is as important as the result.

The writer is not working in a void. However vigorously he protects his freedom to interpret and select, to move and rouse emotion, he must remember that he is part of the community and needs to be vigilant of the power his words may wield. He cannot merely seek to shock or cause misery; if he does, he abnegates the rights due to him as an artist in the community and becomes an irritating appendage to it. Dostoevsky and the Marquis de Sade both wrote vividly about murder. Only one of them was an artist.

I would not pretend that either of my books on the subject rose above the competent, but nor would I wish any reader of mine to imagine that I told the stories of Dennis Nilsen and Jeffrey Dahmer without very careful choices being made. I pondered long and hard over what to include and what to withhold, over how the grisly events should be presented, how much of their detail was germane to an understanding of the wider subject, and how the reader would react to an intimate journey into the biographies and characters of these men.

The writer who avoids responsibility towards his public denies himself one of the severest and most productive disciplines of artistic effort.

Claus von Bülow

If one were to evaluate the success of a film by the amount of furore and media hype it creates, *Reversal of Fortune*, based on the famous trials of Claus von Bülow, must already be a winner. Despite the fact that the film is not released in this country until this month, a myriad column inches have been dedicated to it. The film is undeniably gripping and exciting, and is graced by some fine performances. But what has not been said is that there is something deeply insidious, even dangerous, about it, for in subordinating every consideration to the paramount need to entertain, the film must contain the standard ingredients to make it digestible to an undiscriminating audience. It must have a hero – the lawyer Alan Dershowitz, who with his energetic team of law students successfully appealed against von Bülow's conviction on the charge of attempting to murder his wife Sunny in 1981 by a massive dose of insulin – and it must have a villain – who from the very beginning is Claus von Bülow.

It is not difficult to see what is wrong with this near antithesis: von Bülow was finally proven innocent of all charges against him. Thus the film-makers, in order to have their villain, have contrived to suggest that the jury which acquitted von Bülow must somehow have missed a crucial point. He is depicted as so sinister, so machiavellian, so creepy and cold, that he has got to be guilty of something. The danger lies in the implicit claim that the film industry understands people better than do the courts. "Legally, this has been a very important case to fight," says Dershowitz to von Bülow in *Reversal of Fortune*, "but morally, you're on your own." It is as well to remind ourselves briefly of the facts. Claus and Sunny von Bülow had been married for 14 years when she fell into an irreversible coma at Christmas, 1980. She was immensely rich, bored and unhappy. Her two children by an earlier marriage, Alexander and Ala von Auersperg, were grown up; her child with von Bülow, Cosima, was still a little girl. The two older children employed private detectives to gather evidence against their stepfather, and he was accordingly charged on two counts of attempted murder – the first count referring to an earlier coma Sunny had suffered at the end of 1979, and from which she had recovered. The evidence brought by the prosecution amounted to hostile testimony from Sunny's maid and Claus's mistress, plus medical records which purported to show Sunny's body contained 14 times the safe amount of insulin. There was, too, a needle found in Claus's little black bag, a needle allegedly encrusted with insulin. Von Bülow was found guilty and sentenced to 30 years' imprisonment.

There followed the appeal, dealt with in the film, which led to a second trial in 1985, at which von Bülow was acquitted. He was acquitted not merely because the jury believed he was not guilty as charged, but because it was conclusively demonstrated that no attempted murder had taken place. There was no insulin on the needle, no insulin in Sunny von Bülow's body, the needle had never been used on anyone, there was simply no case to answer. All this, which comes after the events covered by the film, needs to be looked at more closely.

The hypodermic needle was encrusted with Valium and phenobarbitone, not insulin. The blood and urine tests on

Sunny revealed no presence of Valium, but a large quantity
of phenobarbitone, so large in fact, that had it been injected
it would have had to be diluted with one and a half litres
of distilled water and would have left a wound the size of
a cricket ball. No such wound existed. Had the needle been
used on anyone, with whatever solution, it would have been
clean, as the outside surface of a needle is cleaned by human
tissue when it is extracted from the skin. The only way that
the needle could be so encrusted was to have dipped it in a
solution and allowed the solution to dry on it. (This piece
of evidence is mentioned in the film but not developed.)

The doctor who examined Sunny when she was admitted
to hospital during the first coma in 1979 diagnosed that
the coma had been caused by her choking on her own
vomit, thus cutting off the oxygen supply to the brain.
In the second trial he testified that the prosecution in
the first trial had warned him not to volunteer his diagnosis as to the cause of this coma.

Three weeks before the second (and final) coma, Sunny
had again been admitted to hospital suffering from an
acute overdose of aspirin. She had taken a minimum of
67 tablets, possibly as many as 110. It is obvious that such
a large amount of pills can only be swallowed voluntarily,
and it is scientifically certain that they were taken more or
less simultaneously and not over a cumulative period. Had
this been known at the first trial, with its implication of an
attempt at suicide, there might well have been other views
as to the cause of the second coma.

Furthermore, a matter of days before the start of the
second trial, a second needle was discovered in a box on
Claus von Bülow's side of the bed at the family home. It was
seen there by prosecutors and by the journalist Dominick
Dunne, who subsequently wrote two long articles on von
Bülow for the American magazine *Vanity Fair*. How and
why this needle should mysteriously appear four years
after Claus von Bülow had last been in the bedroom, and

after exhaustive searches prior to the first trial, was never explained, but the prosecution decided not to present it in evidence, giving the reason that it would inevitably cause a delay. Nor did they disclose it to the defence, because they deemed that it was not exculpatory and would not therefore be of benefit to the defence (in which case they would have been bound to disclose it).

Finally, medical evidence in the second trial established the cause of Sunny's final coma. It is complex and therefore of little interest to daily newspapers, but it amounts to this: Sunny suffered from reactive hypoglycaemia which lowered her blood sugar count; a large consumption of alcohol combined with eight Inderal tablets acted as a beta blocker which prevented her body from raising the blood sugar to a more normal level, and she descended into the hell of non-life in which she still, ten years later, languishes. There was never any insulin and never any attempt, by anyone, to induce a fatality.

That is the truth of the matter, but it is dull. An innocent man is a less compelling character in a movie than one whose innocence is held in serious doubt even by those who defend him. The director Barbet Schroeder was fascinated by the dilemma of a man, held to be morally despicable, who is none the less innocent of the criminal charges brought against him. It was therefore important that the film should show Claus von Bülow to be morally despicable, to accuse him of being himself, since he could no longer be accused of being a murderer-by-intent.

Reversal of Fortune is scattered with clues as to the film-makers' purpose. One of the defence team at first refuses to be involved with a scheme to enable von Bülow to "escape" from the verdict of the 1982 jury. Another says "Is he the Devil? Can the Devil get justice? Is all this legal activity in Satan's interest?" Only in the closing moments of the film does Sunny's voice, as narrator of her own tragedy, reveal that Claus was indeed acquitted on all

counts in 1985, but adds that no one will know for sure
what happened on that night at the end of 1980, thus
allowing the audience to harbour doubts.

Further doubts are sown by innuendo. At the time of the
trials von Bülow's accusers hired the services of a public
relations firm to spread gossip and damage his reputation.
Some of the rumours then circulated pop up again in the
film.

For instance, it is hinted several times that von Bülow's
primary interest is to enjoy the wealth of his extremely rich
wife. He is shown as greedy, arrogant, tactless. If she dies
he would inherit $14 million. While she is comatose, he is
still able to spend her money like confetti. It was certainly
foolish to be seen living in grand style, with a new and
rather vulgar mistress sharing the relentless limelight, while
one's wife merely breathed, alone, in a hospital bed. But
insinuations are misleading. Von Bülow's defence costs
were paid, initially, by J. Paul Getty Jnr., whose support
never wobbled. Getty had known von Bülow since the
days when he had worked for his father, old man Getty,
throughout the 1960s. Von Bülow was able eventually to
repay Getty (on his own unpressured initiative) by selling
at auction those items of furniture and paintings from the
matrimonial home which had originally been his before
marriage, and which fetched more than $6 million.

Before her death in 1984, Sunny's mother had made a
new will, leaving her fortune to Sunny's two elder children and cutting out Cosima von Bülow entirely. For
three more years Claus fought on behalf of his daughter
to secure parity (i.e. one-third of the total), waiving any
matrimonial or inheritance rights for himself in exchange
for an equitable arrangement for Cosima. He additionally proposed that Cosima's share of the family fortune
be placed in escrow until after his own death, in order
that he should not profit indirectly. The Auerspergs were
initially reluctant, conceding ever larger percentages only

gradually, but von Bülow did win justice for Cosima in the end.

Part of the peace settlement between von Bülow and the Auerspergs is a promise by all sides to cease dealing with journalists. In Claus von Bülow's case, the restriction should prove a blessing, for his experience with publicity has shown a naivety and gullibility remarkable in one supposedly sophisticated. He belies the cliché that all publicity is good publicity, as in his case it has tended to make him seem more detestable than before. Arrogance and grandiosity appear to emerge from every syllable he utters, so it is just as well he can utter no more.

One does not have to like the man. Many people clearly do not – they queued up to denigrate him for the *Vanity Fair* articles. One does not have to share his tastes and values, nor succumb to that rich man's charm which cannot fail to be condescending and which is miles away from the effortless ease of the nobleman. He need not be saintly or brilliant in order to be innocent. What is disgraceful is that Claus von Bülow should be made monstrous to satisfy a media need for explicit monstrosity, that he should be painted in lurid colours because a tragedy occurred and the public mind is deemed incapable of understanding a tragedy without a villain. The von Bülow that the press has created, and which this film endorses, is a piece of artifice, a confection, a character from the *commedia dell'arte*. The real von Bülow is perhaps less sensational – Trinity College, Cambridge at 16, graduate at 19, chambers with Lords Hailsham and Diplock, a passion for architecture and opera – but he is innocent of terrible charges, and his name still carries the guilt.

Harpers & Queen, January 1991.

The Silence of the Lambs

Of course, it is essential that we be made to understand the mind of a serial killer, if only the better to understand ourselves. We must not be permitted the cosy excuse that the killer is different in essence, that he is an alien monster removed from the human condition whom we can contemplate from the safe distance of normalcy.

Killing for enjoyment is, after all, not *in*human at all. Would that it were. It is, alas, a badge which our species wears with shame, and it is right that we should examine why and how it distinguishes us from virtually every other creature on earth.

Psychiatric insights have helped in recent years to unravel the mystery of the homicidal maniac bent on destruction, to demonstrate that he is an extension of ourselves, a postulate of human possibility rather than a denial of what is right and good in the human character. But knowledge derived from psychiatric investigation is necessarily flabby on the moral level. The good doctors may explain, but they do not, and do not wish to, offer guidance. Nor, mercifully, do they seek to entertain. Psychiatry enables us to peek into the grim, dark tunnels of our soul, but it is up to us whether we shudder or are seduced by what we see.

It is when the activities of serial killers are presented as entertainment that real danger lurks not far beneath the surface. Last year, John McNaughton's film, *Henry: Portrait of a Serial Killer*, was refused a licence for public showing in this country. It portrayed the hero, without even a hint of comment, as a bland, featureless young man who murdered as a matter of routine, when the mood took him, in a sequence of attacks notable for their escalating horror and Henry's chilling indifference.

The film showed that killing someone was a long and messy business, and the audience was spared no detail. Just as Henry was morally myopic, so the audience was invited to watch and wonder, but not to judge. No explanations or insights were offered, merely a spectacle of wickedness which, implicitly, we were meant to enjoy.

If you saw the film and came away dazed with the awful recognition of truth, as a kind of catharsis, all well and good. But there was the equally terrible possibility that, without guidance, you might be contaminated by it. *Henry* did very well in New York.

Now there comes another film, even more insidious because well-made and gripping, which depicts the serial killer as genius. *The Silence of the Lambs* is adapted from a paperback thriller by former crime reporter Thomas Harris, whose earlier, second novel – *Red Dragon* – was made into the disturbing 1986 film *Manhunter*, in which, in order to outmanoeuvre a psychopathic killer, the hero has to find the psychopath in himself and is helped on his road to destruction by a machiavellian doctor.

The film was a vivid parable of the very notion of contamination, of trying to understand without a moral rope to cling to. The same doctor turns up in *The Silence of the Lambs*, but now he is elevated to the rank of super-intelligent guru. His name is Dr Hannibal "The Cannibal" Lecter.

The FBI is floundering in its search for a serial killer, nicknamed Buffalo Bill for his tendency to skin the bodies of his victims. There is only one man who can point them in the right direction, and that is Hannibal Lecter, himself in prison for murders of a singularly horrible nature. One of his victims was a musician in the Baltimore Philharmonic Orchestra, whose body was found minus its pancreas and thymus. These organs were served up by Lecter in a dinner he gave the following day for the conductor and president of the orchestra. He is also capable of swallowing eyeballs.

To make matters worse, Lecter was a practising psychiatrist and this victim had been one of his patients.

Lecter displays all the characteristics we have learned to recognise in this kind of psychopathology. He is civilised, articulate, manipulative, proud of his superiority and teasingly sarcastic. He still contributes learned articles to medical magazines and is always several steps ahead of anyone who attempts to categorise him. He is played with hypnotic candour by Anthony Hopkins, as a man whose freedom from moral restraint makes him enticingly glamorous, deliciously attractive.

He even taunts the FBI officer who is sent to interview him, Clarice Starling (Jodie Foster), with the inadequacy of her approach to people like himself. "You've given up good and evil for behaviourism," he says. His own evil is an attribute in which he mischievously glories, playing with his adversaries; criminal psychiatrists call this "grandiosity". He is so sophisticated, indeed, that his company is itself a threat of pollution. After her first interview with him, Officer Starling "felt an alien consciousness loose in her head".

I have reason to know about this danger of infection, for in my many interviews with mass-murderer Dennis Nilsen in the preparation of my study of his case, I found myself beguiled by his humour and intelligence, and begged the police to show me evidence of his crimes to remind myself of what he had done. I needed to see police photographs in order to rescue myself from sympathy. I wanted to understand, not to forgive, still less to condone.

A still more graphic illustration of the power of evil was the telephone call I received from one of Nilsen's victims, whom he had tried to kill but failed, and had then spent 36 hours nursing back to health. I had not interviewed this man when writing the book, as I did not wish to intrude. Two years later he contacted me, unsolicited, and asked if I could place him in touch with Nilsen as he would like to see him again.

The Silence of the Lambs – scheduled for West End release on 31 May – is the hit of New York. Entire audiences are being seduced by the fictional Dr Hannibal Lecter into smothering their moral perceptions. It is not their sympathy which is being invited, but their admiration for his diabolic cleverness.

I wrote "diabolic" with care. I am not a religious man, but it seems to me that if the Devil is to succeed, he must block our legitimate wish to understand, and replace it with an intoxicating acknowledgement of his own magnificent cunning. If thousands of cinemagoers are simultaneously in his thrall, then the notion of contamination through entertainment has reached a new peak.

Evening Standard, 7 March 1991.

Murder as entertainment

Michael Winner is obviously not frightened by controversy, or he would not court it so frequently. He is about to narrate a new television series about police investigations called *True Crimes*.

The first of these, to be screened on Saturday, is a dramatisation of the murder of Oxford student Rachel McLean a year ago. Winner described the programme as "entertainment", although he later revised his opinion and said it was simply "interesting".

In an interview with the *Evening Standard* last night, Rachel's parents said that although they had given permission for the programme they were distressed by the depiction of their daughter's murder. They also observed that the public can barely tell the difference any more between real-life crime, with all its tragic, human consequences, and "entertainment".

"It is true that is how people see crime," said Mrs McLean.

The makers of *True Crimes* are not the only ones to recognise that crimes, the more lurid the better, sell. The Milwaukee murderer Jeffrey Dahmer was convicted barely three months ago, after a trial which revealed horrific details about his behaviour towards the 17 young men he had slain.

Yet already he has been glamorised by his portrait being included in a collection of notable people, and a graphic artist has reduced the narration of his crimes to a strip cartoon, dismemberment and all. The families of those who died are understandably furious.

Winner's doltish insensitivity has none the less drawn attention to a problem which is not easy to resolve. It has two aspects. One concerns the nature of the public appetite for the grim chaos of actual tragedy rather than a tidy fictional rendering of it, and the other involves the responsibility of the artist in satisfying this appetite.

We must not shirk the fact that we ourselves are the audience: the creeping realism of true crime drama answers an unacknowledged need to experience, at one remove, the primal urges of human conduct which civilisation has happily smothered. The staggering popularity of seemingly mundane programmes like *Crimewatch*, which relies on police reconstructions of crime, testifies to this.

There is nothing inherently wrong in our being made to face that part of ourselves which delights in nastiness, providing it is to a purpose. Dostoevsky's *Crime and Punishment* compels the reader to think about the hollow gratuitousness of murder and the damage it does to the soul.

It reinforces the value of those inhibitions which keep wild, undisciplined human nature in check by making the reader feel what it is like to have the hands and mind of a murderer.

On the other hand, the cult movie, *Henry: Portrait of a Serial Killer*, tells one nothing except that murder is a long and messy business. It appeals to that buried fascination simply by gratifying it, and the film is no more than a masturbatory fantasy.

The danger lies in losing the distinction between the two. Anyone who dares depict a true crime in writing or on film must grapple with this question of artistic intent.

A film about the death of Rachel McLean would be justified if it showed the pity of a life snuffed out by sudden uncontrolled jealousy (*Othello* is, after all, a useful play) or even the meticulous detachment of police detection. But if it simply titillates, then it causes distress to the murdered girl's family without any concomitant public instruction to compensate.

Mr Winner describes the case as interesting. It ought to be more than that. It ought to be illuminating and important, or it should be left alone until the main characters are no longer here to be hurt by it.

Oscar Wilde once famously declared that morality had no place in art, that there were only good books or bad books. But when art fashions reality, the responsibility of the artist towards the integrity of his work cannot be evaded. He must juggle with the demand for realism and his onus to reflect or instruct his audience. If he aims no higher than to entertain, then he should stay within the confines of harmless fiction.

There are instances where a certain degree of intrusion might paradoxically assist the purpose of detached reflection. When I wrote an account of the Nilsen case ten years ago (*Killing for Company*) I initially intended not to identify the victims of his crimes, but to list them by number.

Though they had been named in court, I thought it unnecessary to add to the distress caused to their families by parading their suffering before the reader. It was pointed out to me that the reader would be more likely to feel the awfulness of lustful killing and to ruminate upon the terrible disintegration of the personality of the murderer if he knew something of the victims.

The murderer had depersonalised them, treated them as objects or props in his distorted fantasies. It was important to revivify them if the reader was to share in the pity of their deaths. To leave them as numbers would be to collude with the murderer.

Tragically, for Rachel McLean's family, the disaster which befell their daughter propelled her into the public domain. She belongs not only to them, but to the history of criminal aberration. In that sense, a book or film about her fate might just be for the public good.

If it is well-dramatised, it may well so touch the heart as to give vent to grief and compassion, and the family might derive some small consolation from the usefulness of such an exercise. A still photograph of the victim would suffice to identify her.

But if Rachel's death is reduced to a shallow entertainment, it would be a poor excuse for artistic endeavour. And if an actress is actually made to reproduce her terror in order to excite the base voyeurism of the viewer, it would be nothing short of disgusting.

Evening Standard, 2 June 1992.

The Krays film

After watching this film I have overthrown an ideal I have cherished and protected against every attack for more than 30 years: that in no circumstances should a man be murdered by conscious decision of the State in revenge for a murder he has himself committed. If Ronald Kray really was as vile as he is herein depicted, he should have been put to death and swiftly forgotten. It is a tribute to the makers of *The Krays*, to its director and cast, that it should have such a profound effect. It does not manufacture heroes. Nor does it sanitise the violence. Even "violence" is too familiar a word, used to describe the acts of football fans or punches from pickets. When you see our Ronnie slicing the lips and nose from a man he has taken a dislike to, and relishing it, then you know what violence really is.

Still, I do not believe these scenes of cruelty are there to titillate or entertain. They reflect quite accurately the rough intimidating East End world which nurtured the Krays and made their brutish power possible. East London during and just after the war is lovingly portrayed, with an eye and ear for detail which strike a nostalgic chord. The milk bottle on the kitchen table, the women knitting and despising their menfolk with brilliant bitter humour, the crowded nights in the Underground station, all capture that incomparable spirit of the Londoner, and of one glorious Londoner in particular – Vi, the courageous mother of the Kray twins.

Violet Kray is the heroine of this film, and she is played by Billie Whitelaw with a warmth which is completely credible and endearing. She gave her twins absolute love and loyalty, and received in return their respectful obedience. She deserved better than that they should grow into thugs, and they ultimately let her down by disappointing her dream of two perfect boys. Director Peter Medak makes the camera focus on Vi's fierce motherhood, so one understands this was a world dominated by women. Another lingering lament of Auntie Rose (Susan Fleetwood), seated in the armchair face to camera with no gimmicky cuts, is hauntingly moving. And so is the searing shot of Kate Hardie's painful, panicky frustration on an endlessly mirrored staircase. Miss Hardie as Reggie Kray's hopeless little wife, so imprisoned by mindless subservience that her suicide is awesomely logical, is quite astonishing, and the camera spots all its subtleties. Peter Medak uses his camera not as spectator but as commentator, even as mediator.

As the twins, Gary and Martin Kemp are faultless, as powerful in imitation as the Krays were in life, and as thick. Gary Kemp's portrayal of the homosexual psychopath Ronnie is utterly chilling; we are not shown what he does in bed, but it cannot have been much fun for his boyfriend. Martin Kemp is the handsome, human and redeemable Reggie, goaded out of his shred of decency by his mad brother, who watches him murder McVitie in a terrifying frenzy of anger and brotherly affection, stabbing the inert body long after life has left it.

In almost every way *The Krays* is a film to be commended. But it needs some kind of explanation. There are other mothers who bring up boys in wartime without their being brutalised. What went wrong? What is the real source of such vicious emotional death? Philip Ridley's otherwise excellent script does not pose these questions.

Harpers & Queen, April 1990.

CHAPTER 6

The Ethical Debate II

There is another responsibility, yet more provocative and easily misconstrued. It is the responsibility of the writer of true crime towards the subject of his enquiry – the murderer himself.

The relationship between the author and subject, it is generally supposed, ought to be distant and cautious if the subject has strangled a number of people; moreover, if that relationship appears to thrive after the author has finished his work, it may well be suspect.

Such an attitude shows a lack of understanding of what the writer's task should be. It is obviously not to defend, condone or mitigate the awfulness of the killer's crimes, nor yet to present his point of view, which is the job of his defence counsel. Unless he is simply to rehearse the horrifying details of the prosecution's case, for the further enjoyment of the casual reader, the author's purpose must be to investigate beyond the question of guilt or innocence, beyond even the psychiatrist's passion for jargon and categories, and bring his writer's intuition to bear upon the ultimate matter of who this man is, what makes him what he is, how he fits within the scope of human experience and potential. To this end, it is essential that he get to know the subject well, and that a very real degree of trust should evolve between them.

Trust presupposes the banishment of doubt, so that neither the author should worry that he is falling into

the killer's debt and shall have to furnish some reward in
return, nor should the murderer worry that his frankness
might be abused. To take the first point, Dennis Nilsen
was aware of this danger from the very beginning.
Once he had agreed to co-operate in my attempt to
explore his criminal career, he made it perfectly plain
that he should derive no financial advantage whatever
from my book. I have to say that, had it been otherwise, I should have withdrawn from the enterprise,
but in fact I did not have to raise the matter; he
did. He told me it would be wholly improper for him
to profit in any way and, to remove any possible
vestige of doubt, he legally assigned to me copyright
in all his writings up to and including the last date
of his trial, which meant that the volumes of exercise books filled in prison, as well as the infamous
drawings, immediately and irrevocably became my property, to use howsoever I wished.

(The assignation was quite dramatic in itself – as Nilsen
signed the papers within the last half hour before all visits
prior to the trial ceased – and involved my leaving the
prison to call the Governor from a call-box to remind
him that he had given permission for the signature to
be made, but had forgotten to inform the warders on
duty, who tried to prevent it. Had the Governor not been
there to take the call, Nilsen's papers would not have
become mine before the end of the trial, and would doubtless have found their way into whichever newspaper office
offered the biggest booty.)

What did Nilsen gain in return, if not money? I have
occasionally sent him five pounds for some batteries, when
his radio dries up. Like any other prisoner, he is permitted a severely limited amount of private cash. I once
sent him a synthesiser, on which he has composed some
music. These are sporadic, unheralded, small events. There
is no "contact" and I am under no formal obligation, but

perhaps Nilsen was percipient enough to see that this kind of continuity after his conviction was far more valuable than any hidden percentage from my publication. If so, he got what he bargained for.

The second point is that the author should be patently honest when talking to the murderer about his treatment of the subject matter, even if (or especially if) he finds that his view is changing. Authors who flatter their subjects in order to win their co-operation, only to traduce their every word when they go into print, are guilty of base cant and hypocrisy. You do not lie, even to a murderer, and the murderer's crimes, however hideous, do not absolve you from decency in your dealings with him. The article which follows addresses this very problem, as it emerged from Janet Malcolm's study of the MacDonald/McGinniss affair, in which an author felt free to lie as much as he liked to gain a defendant's trust, to serve the "greater good" of the book which was to come out of it all.

I also look at the problem which may arise if the subject proves to be a bore, unequal to the dazzling expectations one has of a central character in a best-seller. Should the author embellish the truth to make it more enticing? Is that not what the French classicists did in their adherence to the principle of vraisemblance? My reference to this principle is, I now think, a little misleading. *Le Vraisemblable* is not that which is probable as opposed to that which is true, but that which is more likely, in the round of human experience and observation, to find an artistic route towards the deepest truths of human nature. Thus Monsieur Jourdain, in *Le Bourgeois Gentilhomme*, is not meant to be taken as totally vacuous as he is written, but to represent the ultimate in the idea of vacuity as it may be revealed in obsessive behaviour. Is the author of a true crime account justified, therefore, in making his villain more villainous, more the emblem of abstract villainy than an unreconstructed portrait of a criminal?

There is one final collusion that I have not examined, which concerns the subtle and nebulous control of sources. A novelist is in absolute control of his fictional creature, whereas the biographer depends upon the material available. Though Nilsen wrote voluminously, and though I used only one-twentieth of what he wrote down, nevertheless I could only work with what he chose to remember, supported by outside research where possible (which always, by the way, corroborated). To that extent, Nilsen determined the parameters of the subject, and I how to work within them. He had no idea, however, that I would try to delve into the history of Scottish fishing villages and the character and mentality of their peoples over the centuries, which made his odd personality accessible on levels more allusive than the direct.

One cannot deny that some collaboration is inevitable; it is the natural corollary of trust. But collaboration is not complicity.

The alacrity with which some agents and TV stations, especially in America, nowadays bid for rights to the "story" of a criminal suggests something far worse than complicity. Perhaps the most blatant example surrounds the case of the first female "serial" killer, Aileen Wuornos in Florida. Rumours abounded of police officers engaged on investigation into her crimes negotiating deals with media representatives even before charges were formally brought against her, and of lawyers charging large sums for the privilege of an interview. Nor was she by any means unique in this respect, as money is frequently offered within hours of a person's arrest, to his or her family, to witnesses, to neighbours, to virtually anyone who can provide exclusive access to an "angle" or first-hand account. The notion that the profitability of dramatic reconstruction may entirely suffocate intelligent perception of the drama itself is malodorous in the extreme, and those who tacitly support it with an expense account conflate the ethical transgression of complicity with the murderer with that other transgression, mentioned in the last chapter, of indifference towards the audience. Ethical considerations are banished to a void, and in their place we find the arid exigencies of the market-place.

That consummate interviewer, Tony Parker, prised open the consciences of 12 murderers years after their convictions and revealed depths of distress the public is generally reluctant to believe. A review of his book, *Life after Life*, concludes this chapter on a note of compassion for those who live with the memory of their appalling acts. No ethical attitude worthy of the name should preclude pity for the wicked.

The writer too can kill: McGinniss v. MacDonald

The question I am most frequently asked about Dennis Nilsen, the serial killer whose case I studied in *Killing for Company*, is whether or not I regard the man as a friend. It strikes me every time that there is an anticipated answer implicit in the question. Of course it must be "no", mustn't it, as there would be something morally repellent in being friends with a man who chopped people up and flushed them down the lavatory. Well, to be honest, the answer has to be "yes", on various levels. Nilsen trusted me with the narrative of his feelings and the exposure of his wickedness; I spent hours and hours talking to him both before and after his conviction; we have corresponded for years; I have been his only visitor since imprisonment; heavens, I even had to lend him a tie to wear at his trial.

How could I describe that relationship as anything but "friendly"? This is not to say that he is the sort of man whose society I would seek in normal circumstances – far from it. But the bond that developed between us, and which I encouraged for professional reasons, that of author and subject, is one that also carries certain responsibilities. After seven years I still visit him. To those who appear horrified at such cavorting with evil I must reply that the alternative, namely to dump him once the fruits of his co-operation had been exhausted, my book published, sold and applauded, would be far more reprehensible. The trust of a murderer, a psychopath, a brute, is no less valuable than the trust of anyone else, and the chief responsibility arising from the acceptance of such trust is not to scorn it.

I am put in mind of all this again by Janet Malcolm's excellent study of the case fought in the American courts between Jeffrey MacDonald and Joe McGinniss, *The Journalist and the Murderer*. MacDonald was tried for the murder of his wife and children. McGinniss undertook to write a book on the case, and to this end he secured MacDonald's complete co-operation, even so far as attending meetings with his defence counsel and using his apartment. The two men were inseparable, virtually living together. MacDonald was found guilty and imprisoned. McGinniss told the convicted man's mother that he would not rest until her son was acquitted, and he wrote letters to him in gaol condemning the verdict as unjust (and incidentally warning him against speaking to any other journalist). When his book *Fatal Vision* was launched, it turned out to be totally opposite to the one he had told MacDonald he was writing, and MacDonald was depicted therein as a cold, ruthless killer utterly devoid of normal human responses.

MacDonald brought a lawsuit against McGinniss, claiming that he had lied and cheated. It was the first time the subject of a book had ever sued the author for saying unflattering things about him, and the jury's verdict in

MacDonald's favour carried severe implications. They said, more or less, that they found McGinniss's betrayal and duplicity as monstrous as MacDonald's crimes. "How can you like a guy who has killed his wife and kids?" asked McGinniss in court. The jury replied, in effect, that you don't have to like him but you are wrong if you lie to him by pretending to.

There are many writers who disagree profoundly with this view. Joseph Wambaugh testified in court that the only responsibility he acknowledged was to the book, and not to any one individual. He said that writers must retain the freedom to lie in order to get the material to make a work of art. Morality does not come into it, he asserted. John Pearson, whose book on the Kray brothers, *The Profession of Violence*, destroyed their last hope of being seen as colourful East End sportsmen, told me, "To be writing a book about somebody is not a normal social situation, and cannot be governed by the normal rules of social intercourse. It is more serious than that." Pearson did not tell the Krays that he was going to reveal them as thugs, and feels no regret; he had a duty to tell the truth as he saw it. As Janet Malcolm neatly puts it, "the whole future of journalism may depend on the writer's freedom to dissemble, because otherwise the subject will flee." By this reckoning, behaviour which we would rightly find objectionable in "ordinary" people is perfectly acceptable if the offender happens to be a writer or journalist, because the book – the printed word – is the greater good. The jury in the McGinniss trial, all of them "ordinary" (i.e. not writers), did not agree that morality was thus flexible.

It was furthermore suggested that the most hallowed of principles, freedom of speech, was itself placed at risk by the McGinniss verdict, and that journalists would be muzzled if the practice became a habit. This is, of course, nonsense. Nobody proposed that McGinniss's freedom to write what he wanted should be curtailed, only that his freedom to act fraudulently be checked. Only a weak or bad journalist has to tell lies to get confidences, and if he is dragged into the court for so doing, he cannot slip behind the curtain of free speech. The freedom to be a hypocrite is not worth protecting. There is a more subtle way in which the writer may be seduced into betraying his subject. People in life are generally much less interesting than people in fiction (to reverse a hackneyed and wrong-headed truism). They are hesitant, inconsistent, muddled, often downright dull. What if the writer discovers his subject is boring? Murderers are notoriously banal people, with scarcely one item of fascination to grip the reader, apart that is from the act of murder itself. I was, in a way, lucky with Nilsen, in so far as he is articulate and has a vivid pictorial memory. MacDonald appears to be the usual type of killer – numbingly trivial and obsessed only with his innocence. McGinniss may well have suffered the awful realisation that if he were to present his subject as he intended, as the lonely innocent wrongfully accused, the reader might be so unimpressed as to shut the book. Horrors! To keep his readers he had therefore to construct a more interesting person as his central hero, namely a monster whom it is easy to contemplate, in all his gory Turkey-carpet colours, as somebody fascinatingly *different*. Jeffrey MacDonald just would not have worked, in literary terms, had McGinniss been honest about him. He had to be invented. Again, it is the book that is the greater good.

Finally, it is said, the writer needs to improve on the truth itself, as that elusive abstract simply does not reside in accuracy. The French classicists understood perfectly well that what was *probable* held more of ultimate truth within it than what was factually *true*, for it represented, in narrative form, one or more of the essences of the human predicament. But a journalist interviewing a subject is not Molière or Racine, and his kind of truth must be more prosaic. He is simply not at liberty to embellish his story with imaginative fancy, however "true" the insights thus furnished to him might appear to be.

Writers of non-fiction are obliged to be far more scrupulous than novelists. They simply cannot regard themselves as having an Olympian licence to make things up. Truman Capote famously wriggled out of this restriction with *In Cold Blood* by having it both ways – making things up and calling the book a non-fiction novel. We should be clear as to what he did. He took a murder case in the Midwest, with two defendants, then used their story as the basis for a novel in which the real case and the real defendants were named, but conversations between them and events in their lives were imagined. He also lied to them about his intentions; they thought he was on their side, which is why they delivered their lives and reputations into his hands, but he cynically watched as they were executed without raising a whisper on their behalf. Capote knew his best-seller depended upon their deaths. This is not to say *In Cold Blood* is not a good book – it succeeds admirably. But it is also wretched. Capote abnegated his responsibility to be honest in favour of a "greater" responsibility to be readable. Wambaugh and McGinniss would agree with him. What none of them will face is that the "greater" responsibility is truly opportunistic, the sight and feel of all those dollars, the sniff of all that fame, the excitement of all that notoriety.

And still the predators swoop. When the Menendez brothers were arrested in Los Angeles on suspicion of the murder of their parents, within *one day* neighbours and school-friends were signed up, a TV film script was commissioned, the boys themselves offered all kinds of promises. There had not yet been any preliminary hearing nor any ruling that there was sufficient evidence to bring a case to trial. The man who started a wild racist witch-hunt in Boston for the killer of his wife, then committed suicide when it looked as if he would be revealed as the murderer,

On Murder

has been ennobled by a book already. It was published here in October. Money is behind all this frantic expedition. Jeffrey MacDonald received 33 per cent of the royalties on McGinniss's book, despite being a convicted murderer and despite the book having traduced him.

Given that everyone knows journalists are not to be trusted, why does anyone consent to be interviewed at all? Further, why do subjects, who ought to be extremely wary, display on the contrary a childish trust and impetuosity, as if they cannot wait to be humiliated and will even connive in their own martyrdom? Janet Malcolm calls it "the old game of confession, by which journalists earn their bread and subjects indulge their masochism." John Pearson ruefully admits that nobody has ever liked what he has written about them. The game continues to be played, although disappointment, even betrayal, are virtually guaranteed.

One sees the principle applied at the moment most entertainingly in the Lynn Barber interviews in *The Independent on Sunday*, which are idiosyncratic and merciless. Sir John Junor, William Hurt, Sir Jimmy Savile, Richard Harris, John Aspinall – her subjects appear to queue up for the mockery. Aspinall says Miss Barber was so sweet when they met, he had no idea she was capable of harshness in print. Yet he is an experienced man, and should have known better. Subjects have none but themselves to blame if they feel let down. They have given in to the transient seduction of a one-night stand.

The long collaboration necessary for the production of a book must needs require a closer friendship between author and subject, and that is when honour and decency should hold sway above the attractions of a quick deception. If the author feels out of sympathy with his subject, he should say so and withdraw. But watch how desperately the subject will use every guile to keep him! I am interviewed, therefore I am.

Harpers & Queen, December 1990

Tony Parker review

Life After Life: Interviews with 12 murderers
by Tony Parker

It is both easy and comforting to point the finger at murderers and declare them to be unlike the rest of us. It makes us feel even safer if we can call them "monsters" and characterise their acts as "inhuman", although there is little clarity of thought behind these labels (labels are there precisely to render thought unnecessary), since murder is an almost exclusively human activity, denied to less refined animals. Presumably that is part of what is meant by Original Sin – the barely tolerable burden of being human is to do wrong knowingly. Murderers are therefore not separate from us, but an extreme example of us, and the burden they carry is correspondingly weightier. If you are beyond persuasion, as are those who think it good to kill killers, then this book will arouse your contempt. But the vast majority of normal people will, I believe, weep several times in the course of reading these astonishing confessions.

Tony Parker's technique is well-known. He has several talks with his subjects, tape-recording the entire conversation. He then edits out his questions, reorders their replies where necessary, and disappears off the page, leaving the subjects to reveal themselves in amazingly vivid monologues. One of his books was devoted to the tenants of a dreary high-rise block of flats; released from the shackles of mediocrity and boredom, they sprang to life, discovering aspects of themselves they did not know they had. Parker can detect gold in a slag-heap. With this new collection, he has found hope amidst the horror of self-hatred.

The 12 murderers who tell their stories are as different from each other as any 12 people can be. Danny killed his grandfather with a pair of scissors when he was 14; Arthur, an acute depressive tormented by feelings of

failure, drowned one of his little daughters in the bath
and smothered the other with a pillow; Andy, a Scot bred
on violence as a banal ingredient of daily life, stabbed a
stranger in the street who looked at him; Valerie killed her
best friend; Philip his 18-month-old son. The names, by the
way, are all invented. It is important to point this out since
those who resent the very idea of murderers being allowed
a voice habitually suggest they all want fame and court
notoriety. Nothing could be less true. These 12 are virtually
anonymous. Moreover, they are all abject in shame.

In each case, what is most frightening is the sheer risible
contingency of these acts, the haphazard way in which they
occur, their lack of solid necessity. They are emblems of
the utter fragility of human existence, its unreason and its
randomness, what Camus called *l'absurde*; indeed his hero
Meursault in *L'Etranger* is just such a murderer, one who
kills because he happened not to do something else. Paul
battered a man to death as he lay asleep in a lodging house.
He didn't know him, had never spoken to him.

> "It could just as easily have been the other way round.
> You know, me the unknown man instead, killed by
> another unknown man . . . It was an absolutely un-
> noticed event."

Danny, the one who killed his grandfather, remarks,

> "I'm sorry he's dead because I liked him, but there it
> is, he's gone and like I said I look on it like it was
> an accident, something that could have happened to
> anyone."

Danny did not have murder in mind. Had a spoon been
lying on the table instead of scissors, had he not been short
of pocket-money, had he not drunk a can of beer, had he
struck the shoulder instead of the neck, all could have

been different, no worse than a commonplace domestic disappointment. A man died, and just as easily he might not have.

William became involved in a brawl with two others who set upon an Irishman; he was stabbed 30 times, slaughtered without mercy.

> "I'd been responsible for the death of someone for no reason, who I'd no personal quarrel with, whom I didn't know, who I'd had less conversation with than I've already had so far with you. What was a fair punishment for that? It's an unanswerable question: all you can say is whatever it was, it was less than I deserved."

It is small wonder that many of these murderers give evidence of that peculiar numbness which psychiatrists term "dissociation", wherein they seem to be spectators of an act perpetrated by someone else. Many of them are still gaunt with wonder that they were able to do such a thing, and fear that they might be capable of it again. (Parker usefully points out in his Preface that 2,500 murderers have been released on licence in the past 35 years, and only ten of these have gone on to kill again.) Versilov in Dostoevsky's *A Raw Youth* observes that it is like having your own double standing next to you. To be aware of oneself, as it were in slow motion, creating death with one's own hands must indeed be a horrible experience. But we are very foolish if we imagine it could never happen to us.

Even the most ghastly account, that of Philip who killed his own baby son, is still recognisably human though it makes painful reading. In a rare editorial intervention, an evidently moved Tony Parker tells us that Philip's eyes were like "caverns of horror" as he remembered his appalling act with raw disbelief even 20 years later. The boy would not stop crying in his cot.

"He'd never liked me and he was doing it deliberately,
so I punched him some more and swore at him. I was
shouting 'I know you don't like me you little bastard.
Tell me you love me. Go on, tell me.'"

Philip threw the little boy on the fire in the grate, then
put him in the sink and poured scalding water on him,
and finally crashed his frail body against the wall. He
doesn't know at what point his son stopped being alive.
Philip insisted on telling the story first, to see if Parker
would still want to talk to him, having heard such vileness.
Now, he looks at young men who would be about his son's
age, and dwells with unforgiving introspection on his own
wickedness. When he was released from prison, he asked
his ex-wife for a photograph of himself with his baby son
taken a few weeks before the murder. He keeps it in a sealed
envelope, precious and safe, but will not open it. He does
not quite say why, but one can see he feels unworthy to
gaze upon it, as if he might contaminate even the picture.

And yet, through all the squalor of human sin, there is
humour, wit, hope and goodness in these pages. William,
entirely uneducated, tuned in to T.S. Eliot and was gradually captivated by the *Four Quartets*, is now married with
a son and happier than he thinks he has any right to be.
Alan, a great towering bully, admits remorse and weeps.

"Inside here it's a hole, a big hollow empty hole, that's
all, a big big hurt. I don't have any excuse for what I
did and there's nothing I can do that will undo it . . .
but Oh Jesus mate how many times I've wished to
God someone'd come along and tell me how I could
. . . If society would only say one day, one definite
day, they'll take me back, that's all I want, for them
to tell me that . . . I'm a big tough man to sit here and
make an exhibition of myself like this crying aren't I
yeh, a really big tough man."

Valerie has turned to religion and would like to work helping ex-prisoners. Andy, the thick-headed Scot, has passed O and A levels inside, having overcome his fear of "textbooks with knowledge inside them". Paul fell in love with the prison psychiatrist, a woman of 57, and now lives with her. Carol pins all her hopes on one meeting with a daughter, now in her twenties, whom she has not seen since she had her adopted after birth.

> "It would be just one nice word: it'd be if she once called me 'Mum'. Just once without even thinking about it. I'm sure that sounds silly but it's the nearest I can get."

When Carol tells how she killed a sailor, she closes with "I'm sorry. That's it. I'm so sorry. I'm so sorry", and one believes her.

These forgotten people, pariahs, pitiful men and women guilty of fearsome acts, here speak with honesty, integrity, intelligence and reflection. Tony Parker's last word, in his acknowledgements to those who went through the experience for him, is "respect". It is a word I echo wholeheartedly.

The Literary Review, March 1990.

CHAPTER 7

Dahmer

Jeffrey Dahmer was arrested in the closing minutes of 23 July 1991, in his neat but disturbing flat in Milwaukee, Wisconsin. The son of a Ph.D. in industrial chemistry, and himself an unremarkable worker at a chocolate factory, his florid fantasy life, which had exploded into the real world with catastrophic results, was to make his name notorious the world over.

I was working with summer schools in Oxford at the time. My involvement began with a call from *Vanity Fair* in New York, inviting me to travel to Milwaukee on their behalf to write a long article on the pending case. I was initially reluctant, both because my duties in Oxford made it difficult for me to leave, and because I knew full well that Milwaukee would be packed with journalists who knew what they were doing, had all the right contacts, and would doubtless have discovered whatever there was to discover. A foreigner would be unlikely to break their united carapace of experience. I feared letting down my editors.

However, I was eventually persuaded, and the resulting piece is the first item in his chapter. To my own astonishment, Dr Lionel and Mrs Shari Dahmer became firm friends, as did Jeffrey Dahmer's attorney (without ever telling me anything I shouldn't know!) and I was able also to move freely amongst the psychiatrists who were to testify in court. The one aspect of this article which I regret is the publication of Dennis Nilsen's letter to me commenting

upon the Dahmer case. Lionel and Shari were angry that
Nilsen should have any opinion at all on a matter which
affected them and their family so intimately, and resented
his contribution. This I fully understood. I had earlier
fought to have the letter excised simply because it confused,
rather than clarified, the issues, but there are exigencies of
journalism which one must finally accept with grace.

The second article, retrospective and a trifle smug I fear,
appeared in *The Times* on the eve of the publication
of *The Shrine of Jeffrey Dahmer*. It is followed by an
interview with me by Charles Nevin.

Dahmer's Inferno

North Twenty-fifth Street is only a couple of miles from
downtown Milwaukee, yet it contrives to feel dislocated,
apart. There is an air of listlessness about the neighbourhood, as if ambition here has been sat upon and the future
is questionable. The small detached houses with verandas
were obviously once pretty, even elegant, but now they
stand like ghosts of a happier time, and you do not walk
down the street without listening for footsteps behind you.

The Oxford Apartments at No. 924 is an interruption
of the street's pre-war architecture, a modern two-storey
building with a cream-coloured façade. It looks, and is,
cheap. Outside hangs a large American flag. When I passed
two months ago, it hung limply at half-mast.

The scene of a crime is nearly always a soul-damaging
place, but almost none in modern American history
compares to the spectacle that awaited police in Jeffrey
Dahmer's small second-floor apartment. For once that
anodyne term "human remains" was horribly accurate.

Apartment 213 contained seven skulls and four heads, three in a free-standing freezer, one in a box on the bottom shelf of the refrigerator. In the freezer compartment of the refrigerator there were assorted body parts. In a blue 57-gallon barrel there were headless torsos, mutilated pieces of human bodies, hands and assorted limbs. There were also more than a hundred photographs of people taken at various stages of dismemberment, most so disgusting that even seasoned police officers could not look on them without feeling faint.

In all, Jeffrey L. Dahmer has been charged with 13 counts of first-degree intentional homicide and two counts of first-degree murder, though he has confessed to having killed 17 men: Steven Hicks, Steven Tuomi, James Doxtator, Richard Guerrero, Anthony Sears, Raymond Smith (also known as Ricky Beeks), Edward Smith, Ernest Miller, David Thomas, Curtis Straughter, Errol Lindsey, Tony Anthony Hughes, Konerak Sinthasomphone, Matt Turner, Jeremiah Weinberger, Oliver Lacy, Joseph Bradehoft. That so many were named within a few days of Dahmer's arrest on 22 July, and all of them since, is attributable not merely to the forensic skills of the Milwaukee County medical examiner but also the confessed serial murderer's own wish to assist in every way towards positive identification.

The Milwaukee City Jail has been a smoke-free zone since July, and Jeffrey Dahmer, a pack-a-day man, is reduced to sniffing smells from the air vents in his cell when prison guards have a smoke. But he is transported by two detectives from the jail to the Milwaukee Police Department one floor below for his sessions with investigating officers, and there he is allowed to smoke as many cigarettes as he likes. (Dahmer is now in the Milwaukee County Jail.)

It is noticeable how subdued Dahmer is now, despite the lack of cigarettes. His confessions are made not in any spirit of bravado or satisfaction, but in abject remorse. His lawyer, Gerald Boyle, is on record as having referred to Dahmer's "anguish". The word may even be too mild to describe the depths of introspective horror which now afflict him.

That a man should be capable of what Jeffrey Dahmer says he has done is in itself a mystery of human destructiveness which is in no way diminished by the spate of "serial killers" revealed in recent years. That he is also in distress, and as appalled as we are by the contemplation of his own acts, compounds the mystery by lifting him from the simple category of a monster whom we can view from a fascinated and safe distance into an uncomfortably recognisable human being. As the scores of journalists who descended upon Milwaukee pieced together Dahmer's history, he gradually emerged as disconcertingly ordinary, even unremarkable, until the secret dissolution of his personality finally erupted upon the world.

We must not treat Dahmer the way he treated his victims, as objects in a fantasy, but must try to inhabit his world, to imagine what it might be like to live inside the head of Jeffrey Dahmer. This is not impossible, for there was a case in England in 1983, so similar in detail, character and motive, as to make one blink in disbelief.

Dennis Nilsen, a highly intelligent 37-year-old civil servant with a penetrating gaze and a dark sense of humour, was arrested in February 1983 and charged with six counts of murder and two of attempted murder. He quickly confessed to having killed 15 men, three in his attic apartment on Cranley Gardens and 12 at a previous address, also on the outskirts of north London. Nilsen worked as an executive officer at a government-sponsored employment agency, and in the evening went to pubs and gay bars for a drink and a chat. Sometimes he took people home with him, and sometimes he killed them. He would wait until they were drunk and sleepy, then strangle them with a tie. (Dahmer gave his victims a drugged drink, strangled them with a strap or his bare hands, and once used a knife.)

Having accomplished this, he would look after the body, care for it, wash and clean it, dress it, put it to bed, sit it in an armchair, and often masturbate beside it. (Dahmer is alleged to have told the police that he once had anal penetration with a corpse.) Some days later, Nilsen would place the body under the floorboards. When the space there became crowded or the stench became overpowering, perhaps several months later, he took the bodies out, dismembered them with a kitchen knife, and burned them on a bonfire in the backyard. Once he was in the Cranley Gardens attic flat, without access to a garden, he sliced the bodies into two-inch strips and flushed them down the toilet (he was eventually caught when the plumbing backed up as a result). The heads were boiled on the kitchen stove. (Dahmer seems to have dissected the corpses almost immediately. He used an electric saw, and acid baths for disposal. The heads were boiled and saved.)

Nilsen referred to the evening of his arrest as "the day help arrived". I first met him two and a half months later, and we had corresponded for three weeks before that. I interviewed him for eight months before his trial, read his own 50-volume prison journals, and wrote a book about his case, *Killing for Company*, published in Great Britain. Nilsen is the first murderer to present an exhaustive archive measuring his own introspection, and his candid, articulate reflections allowed a unique opportunity to enter the mind of a mass murderer, a mind that is frighteningly similar to Jeffrey Dahmer's.

In his "normal" manifestation, Dennis Nilsen is an engaging companion, well-spoken, intelligent and very persuasive. From the letters we had exchanged, I expected someone who was sensitive and introspective. At our first meeting, however, I saw an assertive man, bristling with confidence and swagger, amazingly relaxed as he slouched with an arm over the back of his chair, totally in command and behaving as if he were interviewing me for a job. He gave an impression of intellectual intensity, coupled with a surprising truculence. I soon learned that this was a radical political streak exaggerated by his having to spend countless hours confined with nobody to speak to.

Nilsen is tall, slightly stooped, with a mild but persistent Scottish accent and a natural disposition to hold forth on all manner of subjects. His argumentativeness has frequently brought trouble upon him as a discontented prisoner who is forever pointing out that prison rules should be obeyed by prison governors as well as inmates. His dark sense of humour, too, has often been criticised. During his first interrogation Nilsen, a smoker like Dahmer, asked what he was supposed to do without an ashtray; when told he could just flush the butts down the toilet, he replied that the last time he did that he was arrested. He once told me that if a film is ever made of his case, "they will have to put the cast in order of disappearance."

When I went to see him in August at Her Majesty's Prison Albany on the Isle of Wight (where he is serving a life sentence), to talk about Dahmer's alleged crimes, Nilsen was reluctant at first to address the subject. He looked at me in unaccustomed penetrating silence for a long while, and it was clear that he was contemplating scenes he would far rather banish to the past. Then, in beginning to explain the motivation behind the horrifying deeds he and Dahmer have in common, Nilsen made an observation on the film *The Silence of the Lambs*, a movie about serial murderers which he has not seen, though he knows the book. He said that the depiction of Hannibal Lecter, the dangerous, cerebral killer, is a fraudulent fiction. "He is shown as a potent figure, which is pure myth," Nilsen said carefully. "It is his power and manipulation which please the public. But it's not at all like that. My offences arose from a feeling of inadequacy, not potency. I never had any power in my life."

Eventually, Nilsen was willing, even eager, to examine the case of Jeffrey Dahmer in detail. The comments he made and the letter he subsequently wrote to me, giving his understanding of Dahmer's mind, appear here.

Friday the 23rd of August 1991

Dear Brian,

Thanks for the (all too brief) visit. My first observation of D is that he had two primary social factors working against him. The first is that obviously recurring theme of being "a loner". The second is that (to use the American phrase) he was born on the wrong side of the tracks. I guess that in his most early formative years his immediate household may have been female-dominated (with or without the presence of a passive male adult). As is often the case with serial killers "he always *secretly* wanted to *be someone*" as an adjunct to his lifelong world of fantasy (where he is already powerful and potent). In "real" society he feels that he is a dispensable "nobody" as insignificant as those whose remains adorn his private world (his apartment).

The dichotomy is that his power aspirations are not easily transferable into the real world because he has not been endowed with the overt powers of viable drive and ambition in interpersonal relationships in the real world. He achieves "sexual" fulfilment by acts of power of conquest to render the threatening potency of another man into the absolute and manageable state of passivity. He "fears" the potency of real men because he is by nature a wan and socially shy personality. His needs for feelings of self-esteem are usually satisfied only in his fantasies (imagination) because he cannot garner such fruits from live people. He needs a totally unresisting, passive model of a human being in order to "cross the bridge" temporarily into "society". (Being human he needs "fulfilment" in the human three-dimensional world of real flesh and blood.)

It is significant that a common view of the Stone Age depicts a potent male clubbing a sexually desirable female into unconsciousness and "wedding" her by an act of copulation with her passive body. Here we have the ingredients of power/violence rendering the desired person into a state of extreme passivity followed by sexual release for the conqueror. It is the opposite poles of gross action and gross passivity that attract. This is the constant in the serial-killing conundrum whether the victim is male, female or child. Dahmer's "buzz" comes from the *whole* continuing ritual exploitation of the victim's passivity. Each expressive sequence in the ritual gives sexual and self-esteemed satisfaction. It is a grossly perverted psychosexual act of copulation and like *normal* acts of copulation the satisfaction is of relatively temporary duration. The ejaculation is merely the biological release of inner pressure as is necessary for this human cycle of peaks and troughs.

D is buzzing with excitement and power (his heart rate is pounding at maximum speed) as he "lives out" his omnipotence. (It's the only time in his life when he feels in his fantasies.) This is *while* he is stripping, washing and handling his unresisting spouse. These are all acts of possession and expression of extreme dominance. Perhaps subconsciously he is regressing back to his first (and only) memories of human touch, dependency, security and comfort. (As a very small boy being soiled, undressed, washed, powdered, dressed and "laid out".) After this brief and early period of clear identity and security he drifts away into the wan growing little boy devoid of warmth, touch and comfort. As all humans will do if they cannot satisfy their needs in reality he has drifted to a substitute world where his imagination creates false fodder to feed his hunger. As conditioning advances he finds it less and less easy to relate to other people. Psychologically speaking Dahmer becomes both victim and predator (an easy accomplishment in one's imaginary world). Brian, this is what you described in me as "virile male in performance and passive female in spirit" (an ungovernable mess of contradictions).

His unfolding aberration escalates in accordance with to what degree he is detached from reality (for example, what is termed NECROPHAGY is an extreme example of extreme detachment). This is manifested in "going all the way" in eating the heart of one's victim/spouse. (If you have the power to eat a man's heart this demonstrates your extreme power to possess and his extreme passivity.) The painting and display of the victim's skull is a constant reminder of one's potency.

The paradox is that D cannot hate his victims because his objective is achieved by exercising his will to sexual power and potency. The need is "love" for him and death for the hapless victim. Dahmer is "forced" to unnaturally seek to accede to the demands of his natural instinctive drives. He is perhaps partially aware that his "love" is really for himself or a created entity within his deranged personality. It seems clear that his personality will remain disordered in the absence of a self or presented therapy to help him come to terms with the engine of his acts.

P.S. I'm still in the dungeon.

Jeffrey Dahmer's legal representative is Gerald Boyle, an ebullient, generous man who is recognised all over Milwaukee and always greeted with genuine glee. You feel that people know he is a man of heart, good-natured and generous, and as often happens with those who enjoy life rather than complain about it, he is no longer slim. He is just over 50, but with hair prematurely white, and his Irish ancestry has endowed him with both a sense of humour and a sense of natural justice. His older brother is a Jesuit priest. Boyle himself is a believer without being dogmatic.

Boyle has known Dahmer for three years; they first met in 1988 when Dahmer was charged with child molestation. "It was completely impossible to imagine then," says Boyle, frowning with emphasis and bewilderment, "that he had already killed a number of people. No sign whatsoever. Never once suspected."

Boyle hopes that a proper examination of his client's case may open the way to discern the cause of his tragic torment. "If we can illuminate the condition which afflicts people like Jeffrey Dahmer," he said, "we might have done some little thing for humanity." He has engaged a distinguished forensic psychologist, Dr Kenneth Smail, to report on Dahmer's state of mind.

The facts of Dahmer's case, once stripped of invention and exaggeration, are straightforward enough. ("Forty per cent of what has been printed in the papers is untrue," Dahmer has said recently.) The son of Lionel Dahmer, a chemist, and his first wife, Joyce, Jeffrey was born in Milwaukee but brought up in Bath Township, Ohio, in a middle-class setting. His parents were incompatible and spent so much energy in argument that they had little left to devote to him. They were "constantly at each other's throats," he has recalled. His abiding memory of childhood is of isolation and neglect. He had no close friends, no one with whom he felt at ease and affectionate. He withdrew into a private world wherein he could create his own stories, fantasies that always turned out right as long as no one jostled them.

At Revere High School in Richfield, Ohio, Jeffrey did reasonably well, but was once again noticeably solitary. He played clarinet and tennis, but quite clearly did not belong with any group. Like many friendless children, he took to playing the fool, acting in a bizarre manner to claim attention. According to one classmate quoted in the press, he would bleat like a sheep in class, or fake an epileptic fit. Such are the measures to which the outsider resorts in order to win admission. If that does not work, one can always hijack admission, as Jeffrey apparently did by twice slipping into group photographs of his high school's honour society, where he did not belong. When the photograph was published in the school yearbook in his senior year, his image was blacked out.

Meanwhile, there are reports that he enjoyed skinning dead animals and scraping the meat off with acid. (Many of these reports have come via his stepmother, Shari Dahmer.)

The atmosphere at home had become worse since the birth of Jeffrey's younger brother, David, to whom so much demonstrative affection was offered that Jeffrey was left to draw the conclusion that he was somehow unworthy. Lionel and Joyce finally put an end to their unfortunate marriage in 1978, he having done his best to stay away from her in the last months. They fought bitterly over custody of their younger son. When the divorce was effected, Joyce packed her bags and took off with David, then 12, leaving Jeffrey to fend for himself. He was 18, a morose and sullen figure, heavily hurt by desertion. There was no one to whom he could turn for solace. He was anyway so secretive by then that he never revealed himself for fear that the "self" would be unattractive and misprised. A few weeks later, he picked up a hitchhiker, Steven Hicks, and brought him home. When Hicks said he should be moving on, Jeffrey smashed him in the head with a bar-bell and strangled him, dismembered his body, crushed the bones with a sledge-hammer, and scattered the remains in the woods. Hicks was effectively obliterated, by a man he did not know, because he had threatened to abandon him.

After one semester at Ohio State University, Dahmer dropped out and enlisted in the army for a period of six years. After only two, however, he was discharged under a section of the military Justice Code that covered drug and alcohol use. He habitually drank himself into a stupor. It was yet another way of turning his back upon a world where he felt he did not belong.

At this point, he went to live with his paternal grand-mother, Catherine Dahmer, in West Allis, near Milwaukee, and took a job in a blood bank. By 1985 he was working at the Ambrosia Chocolate Company as a general labourer, a job he held until 15 July of this year, one week before his arrest. He was still a "loner", except that he occasionally brought home young men whom he had met casually at a gay bar. Lionel Dahmer and his new wife, Shari, decided that this was too much for the ageing grandmother to cope with, and said he must leave to find a place of his own. What none of them knew was that, by April 1989, three of the men whom Jeffrey had taken to the house in West Allis never left it.

Dahmer's erratic behaviour had attracted the attention of the law, though not of the homicide squad. State Fair Park police charged him with disorderly conduct in August 1982. He was convicted and fined. In 1986 he was arrested for exposing himself to children; he later claimed that he had merely been urinating and had no idea he was observed. The charge of lewd and lascivious behaviour was commuted to disorderly conduct, and on 10 March 1987, he was found guilty and sentenced to one year on probation.

Then, in 1988, Dahmer picked up a 13-year-old Laotian boy, offering him 50 dollars to pose for photographs. He gave the boy a drink laced with a sleeping potion, and fondled him. Dahmer was charged with second-degree sexual assault and enticement of a child for immoral purposes. He pleaded guilty and was sentenced to eight years, but as he expressed contrition the sentence was stayed to one year's detention and five years' probation, with the eight years suspended upon future conduct (they will now automatically have to be served in full). This meant he could keep his $9.81-an-hour job at the chocolate factory and return to the jail in the evening. He was also to receive psychological treatment to deal with his sexual confusion and his dependence upon alcohol.

That was three years ago. Dahmer is now apparently shocked to discover that the boy involved in this offence

was the brother of Konerak Sinthasomphone, whom he
murdered in May. He had no idea they were related.

Because of a heavy caseload, his probation officer did not
insist on making visits to Dahmer's apartment, but always
consulted with him at her office. He seemed willing and
co-operative. Her reports indicated that Dahmer felt some
guilt about his preference for male partners. His mother,
who had moved to Fresno, California, spoke to him by
telephone for the first time in five years and indicated that
his homosexuality caused no problem as far as she was
concerned.

Two of the speculations which have grown like fungus
since July are that Jeffrey Dahmer hated black men and
despised homosexuals. According to several sources close
to him, neither is true. It has been suggested that he is
homosexual by default – that his sexual orientation was
not a preference but a compensation for the impossibility
of having a relationship with a woman – but in reality he
is a genuine homosexual who has had difficulty coming to
terms with the fact. And he insists that there is no racial
significance in the fact that most of his victims were black.
On the contrary, it is more than probable that he invited
them back to his apartment because he liked them.

A young man named Kenny Magnum was quoted by *The
Washington Post* as saying, "He killed six of my friends,
and you know, before all this, I would have said he was
a regular guy." That, indeed, is the crux of the matter –
Dahmer's "normality". Jeffrey Dahmer is tall, lean, well-
built. Those who have met him say that he looks you
in the eye as he talks, instead of darting glances to the
floor or meditating in the middle distance, as dissemblers
often do. He has a ready smile, but is shy and tentative.
All this relates to the sober Dahmer. Army and work
colleagues have told of his dramatic change of character
when drunk. He would turn aggressive, dogmatic. One
person described how he would become loquacious with

drink, and then tedious, until he felt he had to walk away from Dahmer to avoid boredom.

Neighbours are quoted as saying he was well-mannered and polite, though he kept himself to himself. Taxi-drivers found him intelligent. One of them recalls driving him back from the shop where he bought the 57-gallon barrel which he would subsequently use to dispose of unwanted remnants of his guests.

Other taxi-drivers frequently took him from the apartment to a restaurant called the Chancery, where he would dine alone. Sometimes they picked him up at the 219 Club on South Second Street, a popular downtown gay bar.

That, too, is relatively normal. Though the 219 Club stands anonymously enough on a grim, featureless street where you expect to find only warehouses and used-car lots, once I stepped beyond the simple door, I could have been in Paris or London. Rather than a grim, sleazy, furtive joint with mysterious dark corners and strange smells, it is a cheerful and robustly pleasant place, serving generous cocktails at decent prices and boasting a bright dance floor lit with special effects. Patrons are clean and assertively happy. Jeffrey Dahmer would not look at all out of place in such a venue, and he didn't. One man at the bar, who asked to remain anonymous, told me, "Sure, I saw him in here a number of times. Good-looking guy. I would have gone home with him right away if he'd asked me."

Dennis Nilsen receives one visitor a month. He submits your name to the Home Office and, if it is approved, you arrive on the appointed day at the appointed hour and a guard walks you into Albany prison. After passing through several guard stations and steel doors, you arrive at a small square table in the prison visiting room, surrounded by other such tables, at which prisoners and their girlfriends hold hands and gaze at each other. Guards sit around the edge of the room, but they cannot hear conversations.

Even in his simple prison uniform of blue denim trousers and blue-and-white striped shirt, the same as everyone else, he stands apart, and glances indicate he is recognised. Nilsen thinks his notoriety is a fiction of the press, but that is because he tries to forget the emotional import of what he did, and the rest of us cannot.

When I visited Nilsen recently, he knew that I wanted to ask him for his opinions of Jeffrey Dahmer. He had read several accounts of Dahmer's case in newspapers that warders had left lying around, and had heard reports on BBC radio. Though he was initially reticent on the subject, Nilsen is a perceptive, talkative man with intellectual pretensions, and he was soon willing to analyse Dahmer from his own unique perspective. As usual, he began by taking refuge in humour, moving his chair opposite me "because we don't want anyone to get ideas."

Dennis Nilsen is the son of a Scottish mother and a Norwegian father who met during the Second World War in Scotland and separated soon afterward. He does not remember seeing his father at all, and was brought up by his mother and grandparents. An insecure, melancholy little boy, Nilsen worshipped his adventurous, seafaring grandfather. One day when he was six years old, Nilsen was excited when his mother asked him to come and see "Grandad". She took her son into another room, where a long box lay on trestles, and lifted him up to look inside. In the box was his grandfather. The taboo against the mention of death had disastrous consequences for the boy: the image of the loved one and the image of the dead object were fused.

The confusion of love with inanimate bodies became sexual when Nilsen was eight. He nearly drowned as he waded from a beach near his home into the North Sea; he was rescued by a teenager who then molested him as he wavered in and out of consciousness. (Dahmer's father reportedly told police that when Jeffrey was eight he was

sexually molested by a neighbour boy. Dahmer has said he
has no memory of the incident. His father now says the
assault never occurred.)

At school Nilsen was friendless and, like Dahmer, a
bit of a joker. He spent 12 years in the Army Catering
Corps, where he learned his butchering skills. (Dahmer
learned all about the disposal properties of acid by virtue
of his father having been a chemist.) He also discovered
an alternative to solitary sex: "The novelty of one's own
body soon wore off and I needed something positive to
relate to," he remembered later. "My imagination hit on
the idea of using a mirror. By placing a large, long
mirror on its side strategically beside the bed, I would
view my own reclining reflection. At first always careful
not to show my head, because the situation needed
that I believed it was someone else. I would give the
reflection some animation, but that play could not be
drawn out long enough. The fantasy could dwell much
longer on a mirror image which was asleep." Later, the
fetish involved make-up "to erase the living colour".

After leaving the army, Nilsen lived alone in various
flats in London. Though promiscuous, he was surprisingly
puritanical about the life he was leading. Anonymous sex,
he wrote, "only deepens one's sense of loneliness and solves
nothing. Promiscuity is a disease." Like Dahmer, he felt
guilt about his homosexuality, and he, too, brushed with
the law when he picked up a boy who fell asleep in his
flat after drinking, and woke up to find himself being
photographed. A tussle ensued, but following an interview
at the police station no charges were brought. The camera
is an essential element in both Dahmer's and Nilsen's cases,
for it is one of the props of the florid fantasy life that
eventually swallowed up both men.

Nilsen made one attempt at a domestic relationship,
but it was doomed and lasted only a matter of months.
Dahmer has never had an enduring relationship, though

there was one association that went on for two and a half months. Both men were confirmed outsiders, looking at the real world from an imprisonment not of their own choosing, but which they learned to cherish for want of anything else. "I had always held within me a fear of emotional rejection and failure," wrote Nilsen. "Nobody ever really got close to me ... There was never a place for me in the scheme of things ... My inner emotions could not be expressed, and this led me to the alternative of a retrograde and deepening imagination ... I had become a living fantasy on a theme in dark endless dirges." This may also represent an accurate portrait of Jeffrey Dahmer's frame of mind.

"The loner has to achieve fulfilment alone within himself," writes Nilsen once more. "All he has are his own extreme acts. People are merely supplementary to the achievement of these acts. He is abnormal and he knows it."

Nilsen reached the point where he felt utterly useless and superfluous to society. "Loneliness is a long unbearable pain. I felt that I had achieved nothing of importance or of help to anyone in my entire life. I would think that if I drank myself to death my body would not be discovered until at least a week after (or longer). There was no one I felt I could call upon for real help. I was in daily contact with so many people, but quite alone in myself." (Dahmer is also apparently convinced that, even before the murders, there was no source of pride for him, nothing he could point to in his past with any degree of satisfaction.)

At the end of 1978, Nilsen spent six whole days with his dog over the Christmas period, until he went out for a drink the evening before New Year's Eve and met a young man, whom he invited back. In the morning the man would be leaving. Nilsen decided he would keep him. The man was strangled in his sleep. Thus began what he has disconcertingly called his recruitment of "a new kind of flat-mate". Dahmer is alleged to have admitted that his first victim, Steven Hicks, was killed at the moment when he realised the boy was going to leave. Thereafter the pattern was disastrously repeated, with each departure a threat of abandonment, a death of its own.

In both cases the pattern took some time to establish itself. A whole year elapsed between Nilsen's first murder and his second, some six and a half years in Dahmer's case. Nilsen's frequency of killing gradually escalated into a desperate, unstoppable orgy of panicky destructiveness, with seven men murdered in one year. Dahmer's last four victims died within three weeks. "Each one seemed to be its own last time," wrote Nilsen, who insists that the term "serial killer" is inaccurate because it suggests the *intention* to repeat. "You might as well call Elizabeth Taylor a serial bride," he adds dryly.

It is painful for any of us to survive without a proper sexual and social identity, and for this we need to be in touch, sporadically if not constantly, with human goodness. Both Nilsen and Dahmer appear to have been denied this advantage. They each resisted tactile contact. Nilsen's mother admitted to me that she could not cuddle him as a baby; she wanted to, but he appeared to repel demonstrations of affection. The Cleveland *Plain Dealer* quoted Dahmer's stepmother, Shari, as saying, "He couldn't embrace, he couldn't touch. His eyes are dead."

It is common in semi-autistic children and adolescents to hold this kind of distance, but it is debatable whether the condition is genetic, or whether adults should be held accountable for it. At any rate, it may engender in the long term an unassailable habit of distrust. Dahmer's probation officer noted that his general outlook towards people was "basically mistrusting". In the same interview Dahmer said that if he could change anything in his childhood it would be the way his parents behaved towards each other (he would "change that parents didn't get along").

This ingrained suspiciousness makes it difficult for such people to express any emotion apart from anger, and renders them liable to attribute to others certain attitudes and feelings without checking if they are true or justified. It becomes slightly easier to imagine, then, that Dahmer's victims may have unwittingly stumbled into a private drama in which they played a role foisted upon them by his interpretation of their attitude or indifference. They could not have intuited the deep, frustrated aggression which lay beneath that retiring façade.

Hence the purpose of fantasy in Jeffrey Dahmer's life. He told the police that he had been lost to fantasies from childhood. Even as an infant he had been withdrawn, living privately in his own dreamworld. Gradually, the fantasy life became more important than life outside it, and he emerged only reluctantly to face practical realities. Imperceptibly, the private cherished world of fantasy *took the place of* the real world, diminishing the value he might place on real people.

There is nothing inherently bad about fantasy; indeed, it is very common and quite harmless. To the lonely child it is a solace, and must be welcomed. It may take hold if the loneliness is not relieved in adolescence, however, and grow larger and more complex in adulthood. Once fantasy becomes more *beloved* than reality, it cannot be held in check, and risks breaking through the barrier into real life. People from the real world are often unaware of the terrible danger they run in coming close to such intensity.

This is how Dennis Nilsen expressed the feeling which might have possessed Jeffrey Dahmer: "I made another world, and real men would enter it and they would never really get hurt at all in the vivid unreal laws of the dream. I caused dreams which caused death. This is my crime." And again: "The need to return to my beautifully warm unreal world was such that I was addicted to it even to the extent of knowing of the risks to human life . . . The

pure primitive man of the dream world killed these men
. . . These people strayed into my innermost secret world
and they died there. I'm sure of this."

There is a Manichaean touch to this awful vision which
would come as no surprise to a theological student, for it is
axiomatic that the man imprisoned in fantasy has forsaken
the world of God to pursue his miserable life in the vivid,
seductive, intoxicating world of Satan. (Jeffrey Dahmer's
favourite movie, which he watched again and again, is
Exorcist II, and it would be hard to find many films more
satanic.) It is not at all unusual for murderers to feel that
they are a battleground for opposing forces – darkness and
light, God and the Devil, good and evil – or that they are
two people in one, the "bad" identity being held responsible
for wicked deeds and the "good" one chastising him. To an
extent, this is true of all of us, but the repetitive murderer
illustrates the condition most starkly. "I always covered up
for that 'inner me' that I loved," Nilsen wrote. "He just
acted and I had to solve all his problems in the cool light of
day. I could not turn him in without also destroying myself.
In the end he lost. He still lies dormant within me. Will time
destroy him? Or was he only lost temporarily? When I was
on my high, [my dog] would become sometimes frightened.
She was only a simple dog but even she could see that it
was not the real Des Nilsen . . . She would go off to a quiet
corner and hide. She would greet me the next morning as
though I had been away . . . dogs know when your mind
has been changed in a drastic way."

Dahmer's mind grew so distorted as to require nourishment in death, but the "normal" guy whom people saw in
the street or at the 219 Club disapproved of his conduct.
Dahmer's contrition after his conviction for molesting a
child was genuine enough. In July of this year he issued a
statement through Gerald Boyle, apologising to the families
of the dead "for all the heartache he caused". It would be
facile to dismiss this as simple hypocrisy.

Dennis Nilsen said that at the actual moment of killing he was in the grip of an overwhelming compulsion. "My sole reason for existence was to carry out that act at that moment," he wrote. "I could feel the power and the struggles of death . . . of absolute compulsion to *do*, at that moment, suddenly." He claimed that he had no power of responsibility at the time, and that, afterwards, he was inhabited first by fear, then by "a massive and suppressed remorse". The police had shown him a picture of one of his victims, for identification. "I looked at the photo of Martyn Duffey today," he wrote to me, "and it shocked me seeing him so lifelike in that photo and dead, gone, destroyed by *me*. I can't stop thinking about it. I am . . . amazed that all this – from beginning to end – could ever happen." Dahmer has also recently spoken of "compulsion".

With both men, the agents which facilitate loss of control and smother the inhibitory mechanism are music and alcohol. Dahmer listened to heavy-metal rock bands like Iron Maiden and Black Sabbath, Nilsen to Shostakovich and Abba. Dahmer would use an eight-track player with headphones and retreat into his "own little world"; the second of Nilsen's victims was actually strangled with the cord of his headphones as he was listening.

Nilsen drank great quantities of Bacardi and Coke; Dahmer drank almost anything that was available, but especially beer and martinis. Many witnesses quoted in the press have attested to his extraordinary Jekyll-and-Hyde transformation when drinking. A colleague from Dahmer's army days, David Rodriguez, said, "He's a likeable guy, except when he's drinking he's different." His bunkmate in the Eighth Infantry Division at Baumholder in West Germany, Billy Capshaw, said Dahmer became moody and menacing when drinking. "You could tell in his face that he wasn't joking. It was for real. That's why it bothered me. It was a whole different side. His face was blank." Even his stepmother told *The Plain Dealer*, "He has a terrible drinking problem. It makes him a different person."

Nilsen wrote, "The pressure needed release. I took release through spirits and music. On that high I had a loss of morality and danger feeling . . . If the conditions were right, I would completely follow through to the death."

As a result of this disastrous loss of control, the aftermath of each killing involved a careful reconstruction of self and sanity. Nilsen said that he sometimes could not remember the actual moment of murder, but would find a dead body in the morning and realise that it had happened again. He would then have to walk the dog and go to work as part of his "normal" life. *The New York Times* quoted police sources to give an account of Dahmer's second murder, the first in Milwaukee (this does not appear in the official criminal complaint against him). He met the man at the 219 Club and went with him to the Ambassador Hotel. There they both got drunk and passed out. "When he [Dahmer] woke up, the guy was dead and had blood coming from his mouth." Dahmer then left the body in the hotel room, went to a store and bought a suitcase, returned to the hotel, and put the body in the suitcase. He called a taxi and went to his grandmother's house in West Allis, where he was then still living, taking the suitcase with him.

All this sounds callous and chilling, as indeed it is when all we are required to do is imagine it. If you actually have to do it, it is a devouring nightmare. Dahmer had not killed for six and a half years. He probably thought it would never happen again. Then it did. He had to emerge quickly from the episode of what psychologists call "dissociation" (when he was controlled by fantasy and not by reason), and reassemble his personality on the spot. He had to rediscover his emotion, his feeling, his self, and what he found would horrify him. Most devastating of all would be the knowledge, the near certainty, that he would do it again. To continue living with the recognition that you have the hands and heart of a killer is to walk in a permanent hell. As

the crimes sped up and Dahmer was eventually surrounded
by human debris, his personality teetered on the verge of
total disintegration. There is a tragedy for the people who
died, and another for those who carry death with them.

It is even possible that Jeffrey Dahmer dimly feels some
kind of "shared" tragedy with the victims, as if they have
all suffered from indifference and neglect and are united in
this dramatic denouement. If this is true, it is, pathetically,
the closest Dahmer has ever felt to anyone, and that death
should be required to effect this "togetherness" is an eloquent judgment upon his state of mind. Nilsen very often
identified with the people he killed, *envied* them almost.
Describing the moment of "coming to" after a murder,
he wrote, "I stood in great grief and a wave of utter
sadness as if someone very dear to me had just died . . .
I sometimes wondered if anyone cared for me or them. That
could easily be me lying there. In fact a lot of the time it
was." Elsewhere, he wrote, "I was engaged primarily in
self-destruction . . . I was killing myself only but it was
always the bystander who died." One of the reasons Nilsen
was able to murder so many men was that most of them
were young, single, unemployed drifters – nearly invisible
when they were alive, forgotten when they disappeared.
Of Dahmer's victims, *The New York Times* said, "some
of them were like Mr Dahmer himself, people of whom
society did not take much notice."

We have only to pursue this line of thinking a little
further to tangle with the vexed matters of necrophilia and
cannibalism, both of which may be relevant to Dahmer's
case; for the desire to identify with the victim, to be at
one with him, to share his fate, cannot in the end be more
graphically expressed than by eating him.

Necrophilia is often misunderstood because it is generally
held to mean sexual congress with a corpse, whereas that
is only one manifestation of the disorder. It was certainly
appropriate to John Christie, who murdered six women

in a London house in the 1950s, because he could only
perform sexual intercourse if the women were dead; he
killed them *in order* to have sex with them. But there are
other necrophiles: those who steal corpses and hoard them,
those who like to sleep in cemeteries, and those who find
death beautiful. Necrophiles are difficult to recognise, but
according to Erick Fromm's findings they often have a
pallid complexion (as does Dahmer), and they speak in a
monotone (Dahmer's voice is reportedly almost devoid of
expression or inflection). They are fascinated by machin-
ery, which is unfeeling and anti-human. (Peter Sutcliffe,
the Yorkshire Ripper, played with car engines for hours
on end. Both Nilsen and Dahmer are keen on photography and movies.) They are pedantic about dates and details, i.e., "facts" rather than "feelings" (Peter Kürten,
the Düsseldorf sadist of the 1920s, had precise recall of
murders he had committed 30 years before; this trait also
applies to Dahmer and Nilsen), and see things in black
and white rather than colour (Nilsen called himself the
"monochrome man"). They also feel happy with routine,
however bizarre, because it, too, is mechanical. (In high
school, Dahmer reportedly developed a ritual walk to the
school bus – four steps forward, two back, four forward,
one back – from which he never deviated.)

One kind of necrophile is the "lust murderer", for whom
the act of killing provides excitement: when he felt the urge
and had no victim at hand, Peter Kürten would break
the neck of a swan in the park and drink its blood. But
there is an entirely different necrophile who is appalled by
sadism and entranced by the sight of a dead body. Nilsen's
crimes place him in this category, and Jeffrey Dahmer may
possibly represent a variation of the type. There are stories
of Dahmer's having conserved the corpses of animals when
he was a child, and there is the even more telling admission
that he drugged his victims with a sleeping draft. To the
cynic, this may appear to be the easiest way to ensure

that the victim could not fight for his life, but it may just as readily show that Dahmer loved the look of an inert, unmoving body. He used a drug (Halcion) to sedate young Sinthasomphone, the Laotian 13-year-old whom he fondled in 1988, and made no attempt to kill him.

The *Milwaukee Sentinel* unearthed the interesting information that Dahmer had once been evicted from a gay bathhouse. While other men were intent upon making contact and perhaps having sex, Dahmer would invite a man to his private room and offer him a drugged drink. It happened so many times that he was told not to come back. One of the men was unconscious for three hours. "His interest in me didn't seem to be sexual," the man recalled later. "It seemed to be to get me to drink. Maybe he was experimenting with me to see what it would take to put someone out." It is much more likely that he wanted to gaze upon, and touch, a body which did not resist his attentions. It is like the game of "playing dead", a pretence children use to explore and touch one another's bodies without fear of reprimand.

Dennis Nilsen's experience may offer yet more clues. For him, the dead body was an object of beauty, even of veneration. "I remember being thrilled that I had full control and ownership of this beautiful body," he wrote of one victim. "I was fascinated by the mystery of death. I whispered to him because I believed he was still really in there." Of his last corpse, Stephen Sinclair, he wrote, "I entertained no thoughts of harming him, only concern and affection for his future and the pain and plight of his life ... I had a feeling of easing his burden with my strength ... I just sat there and watched him. He looked really beautiful like one of those Michelangelo sculptures. It seemed that for the first time in his life he was really feeling and looking the best he ever did in his whole life." Later Nilsen said that the man had never been so appreciated before. Nilsen also called his actions "misplaced love out of its time and out of its mind."

The uneasy truth is that necrophilia is often the most extreme perversion of something which is essentially good, the love instinct. In *On the Nightmare*, Ernest Jones divided necrophiles into two types: those who have a "frantic aversion" to being deserted, like Periander, one of the Seven Sages of Greece, who is reputed to have had coitus with his wife, Melissa, after her death; and those who want union with the dead, either to give love and solace or to express hatred. Both categories have their application in Nilsen's case, and both may have something to teach us about Dahmer. Nilsen masturbated over or beside the corpse, and Dahmer has told the police he had "oral sex" with a dead body on more than one occasion.

"I think that in some cases I killed these men in order to create the best image of them," wrote Nilsen. "It was not really a bad but a perfect and peaceful state for them to be in." He experienced "a feeling of oneness" with the corpse. Dahmer has likewise expressed the desire to join somebody, to be "at one" with another person. The most vivid way in which this can be achieved is by taking the flesh of another into one's body.

Necrophagy, or the eating of corpses, is an extremely rare aberration, though some grisly instances of it have been recorded in detail by J. Paul de River, a specialist in the field. It is essentially the most desperate measure to which one may resort in a desire for human contact, and is pitiful as well as repulsive. Jeffrey Dahmer confessed under interrogation that he had saved the heart of one of his victims "to eat later", and there is another report that he placed biceps in the freezer. In effect this was a way of "keeping" someone with him, in other words, a perversion of the romantic notion "to have and to hold".

However ghastly we may find the practice, cannibalism actually has a long history among some civilisations and has often been considered honourable by those tribes which have entertained it as a noble ritual. Indeed, a strong echo still exists in our society, for what is more symbolically cannibalistic than the sacrament by which Christians take the body and blood of Christ into themselves? In this context, it is interesting that Nilsen (who never admitted to necrophagy) frequently uses words like "purification" and "sacred" and "this almost holy feeling" when describing his behaviour towards those who died at his hands. Of his last victim he wrote, "Here in this cell he is still with me. In fact I believe he is me, or part of me."

It is Nilsen's opinion that claims of Dahmer's cannibalism are probably not true. "He is talking subconsciously," Nilsen told me in our recent interview. "It's a kind of wishful thinking. What he really wants is spiritual ingestion, to take the essence of the person into himself and thereby feel bigger. It's almost a paternal thing, in an odd way." Significantly, Milwaukee Police Chief Philip Arreola told *The Milwaukee Journal* early in the investigation that "the evidence is not consistent" with cannibalism, implying that none of the body parts which littered the apartment supported Dahmer's contention.

(Somewhat tentatively, I asked Nilsen if he had ever been tempted to eat parts of his victims. As usual, he used his strange brand of humour to disguise an unpleasant subject. "Oh, never," he replied. "I'm strictly a bacon-and-eggs man.")

When all these fantasies subside, the horror of the real event obtrudes once more. In the days and weeks following his arrest, when Nilsen had been "rescued" from the nightmare of his London flat and forced to ponder upon what he had done, he described himself as "unclean". It was after the 11 days of his long confession to the police that he reached the lowest depths of remorse and self-loathing. "My mind is depressively active," he wrote. "The details of this case are horrible, dark and alien . . . I must be a really terrible, horrific man . . . I am damned and damned and damned. How in heaven's

name could I have done any of it?" There was one particular killing which he could not bear to think about;
when the subject was raised his eyes filled with tears, and
he left the interview room rather than be vanquished by
emotion.

There are again parallels here with Jeffrey Dahmer.
According to several sources, he, too, feels "damned",
beyond redemption, unforgivable. He, too, feels the pain
of having done things more heinous, in his own eyes,
than anyone else. Though he has not been seen to shed
tears, he is known to view with foreboding the likely
retelling of his actions in court.

According to Nilsen, Dahmer would have felt, on his
arrest, an immediate sense of relief that it was all over.
"He couldn't leave his apartment. He was trapped, stuck
in that prison as in a tomb. There was both attraction
and repulsion and at the moment it's repulsion which will
predominate. He will feel an immediate sense of relief that
it's all over, followed by oppressive guilt and shame. He will
need to get through this somehow and find some self-esteem
to help grow towards maturity. Whatever institution he
goes to will be better than the prison he has been carry-
ing around with him, because people will be there, and
he will not be alone any more."

Nilsen also thinks that Dahmer might not have properly
"come out" yet, and that had he felt less ambiguous about
his homosexuality the murders might conceivably not have
occurred. In prison, Nilsen wrote a poem which dramati-
cally confused the notion of killing men as one crime and
loving men as another, with the subtext that guilt for the
latter might be replaced by guilt for the former. The poem
reads, in part:

> Confusion in the fact of being evil,
> "Born into evil, all the time?"
> When evil is the produce

Can there be a doubt?
When killing men has always been a crime . . .

There is honour in killing the enemy,
There is glory in a fighting, bloody end.
But violent extirpation
On a sacred trust,
To squeeze the very life from a friend?

Sentencing the fact of being evil,
Dying of evil all the time.
When love is the produce,
Can there be a doubt?
When loving men has always been a crime.

"When Dahmer lost his job," continues Nilsen, "he lost the only visible means of normality. After that, things could only get worse. Had he not been caught, bodies would have been coming out of the window. He was feeling like an alien in a hostile environment, without any roots whatsoever."

Nilsen's last glimmer of self-esteem was to hold on to his "innocence", by which he meant not to deny that he had killed, but to give voice to the feeling that he had in some way been used by a power to which he had surrendered control. He could see both the angel and the devil in himself, and the survival of his self-regard depended entirely upon his keeping that angel, however tiny and weak, in view.

It sounds as if Jeffrey Dahmer is not yet able to see the angel. He is still in despair, his present position confirming his black view of himself as an outsider whose life serves no purpose, who would be better off dead. And yet he did not rest until he had identified all the victims. The police, unable to make official comment, allow the inference that he was not only co-operative but even helpful. "If I can restore names to them all," Dahmer said, "at least that is something good I can do."

Nilsen talked about Murder Under Trust, "under my roof and under my protection – the most horrible thing imaginable." But it was not the most horrible thing he did. Philosophically and emotionally, we must all recognise that we are capable of killing, but we shrink from the desecration of corpses. When I told Nilsen that it was this which defined the gulf that separated him from the rest of humankind, he remonstrated with me and told me my moral values were confused. His reasoning was that, while it was wicked to squeeze the life out of a person, it was harmless to cut a dead body, which was only a thing and could not be hurt. This was, I had to say, logical but inhuman. Respect for the dead goes beyond civilisation to the very marrow of our bones, to essential concepts of worth and spirit. It may be illogical, but its absence, to the common man, points to madness.

There was one particular day when I forced myself to face this madness, and my life has not really been the same since. I had previously written about eighteenth-century history or twentieth-century literature, and was quite unused to delving into the dark recesses of mental disorder. I found myself at ease with Dennis Nilsen, and asked the police to show me the evidence of what they had found in his London flat, to remind myself of what he had done. They were reluctant, for they knew what disastrous effect the photographs could have. There were two brown cardboard boxes containing photographs of progressive discovery, starting with the house, then the door of the apartment, then the bath, from beneath which protruded two human legs, then the black garbage bags, and the contents of the bags, and so on. I could look at only 12 of them before I was overwhelmed with pity for these poor young men, reduced to refuse. It breaks one's heart, too, to think of little Konerak Sinthasomphone, who tried to escape from Jeffrey Dahmer and was brought back, or of Tony Hughes, the deaf-mute who went trustingly to Apartment 213 and might have found no way to protest what was happening to him. These images enter the brain, and nothing can ever dislodge them.

How could Dennis Nilsen, with quasi-scientific curiosity, inform me that the weight of a severed head, when you picked it up by the hair, is far greater than one might imagine? Clearly, to be able to make such a comment, to dismember the bodies of people he had seen when alive, and to continue living surrounded by their pieces, demonstrates insanity. This is the *res ipsa loquitur* argument – "The thing speaks for itself" – which is circular but correct.

Despite the common sense inherent in the proposition, it is difficult to convince juries of it, because they somehow feel the murderer is thereby being excused. Juries cannot bring themselves to consider that a person can know what he is doing, but have no *emotional* awareness of it at the time: that if the emotional factor is drained from him he is like an automaton. When Nilsen was convicted in 1983, the jury was initially divided down the middle on the question of his mental responsibility, and came back to seek further guidance from the judge, who introduced the non-legal and non-psychiatric concept of evil. "A mind can be evil without being abnormal," he declared. He seemed more certain about the matter than any philosopher since Socrates, and his certainty sent Nilsen to prison rather than to a mental institution.

In the state of Wisconsin, the American Law Institute test of insanity (which has progressed somewhat from the 1843 M'Naghten test) requires that Jeffrey Dahmer show that he suffered from a mental disease or defect which significantly reduced his capacity to appreciate the wrongfulness of his acts, if he wishes to establish non-responsibility for them. A predilection for fantasy over reality and consequent incompetence in determining reality may point in this direction, but there is strong resistance to what has been called "the power of the psychiatric excuse".

My book on Nilsen was called *Killing for Company* for good reason. Dead people became his companions. Most

of them died because Nilsen believed they would soon go
home and he did not want them to. He wished to keep
them, to cherish them, to be with them, so he killed them.
Jeffrey Dahmer has likewise admitted that the decision to
kill was made when his "friend" wanted to leave. On the
day of his arrest, he had 11 "friends" to keep him company
– all skulls or severed human heads. If this does not indicate a mental disease or defect that impaired his ability
to distinguish wrong from right, reality from fantasy, it is
difficult to know what might.

There has been a rash of cases, especially in America, that
postdate the Boston Strangler of the early sixties (Albert De
Salvo), then thought to be a killer without parallel, and
that surpass him in the horror and magnitude of their
crimes. There is every reason to conclude that murderers
like Dennis Nilsen and Jeffrey Dahmer are becoming progressively less rare and may well come to represent a type
of "motiveless" criminal who belongs predominantly to the
twentieth century.

The public does not really want to find the reasons
for this, and who, perhaps, should blame them? They are
content to read a crazy catalogue of odious incidents and
go no further. As I wrote about Nilsen in 1985, sympathy
with murder is unthinkable; it is even safer not to understand. But this craven attitude amounts to abnegation of
responsibility. The murderer takes his place in the jumbled
kaleidoscope of the human condition. So, too, does his
audience. For them to enjoy the display of crime, detection and retribution, while refusing to be drawn into a
steady contemplation of themselves as audience, and of the
subterranean disturbances which the case echoes, would be
fruitless.

Bertrand Russell called Spinoza the noblest and most
lovable of the great philosophers, and ethically the most
supreme. This seventeenth-century Dutch Jew of Portu-
guese descent was despised by Jews and Christians alike

for his lack of prejudice. "I have striven not to laugh at human actions," he wrote, "not to weep at them, nor to hate them, but to understand them."

Vanity Fair, November 1991.

Marks of the Beast

Ten years ago, on 23 February, 1983, Dennis Andrew Nilsen was arrested in Cranley Gardens, Muswell Hill, north London, and charged with a particularly gruesome sequence of murders. This time last year, Jeffrey Lionel Dahmer stood trial in Milwaukee, Wisconsin, on strikingly similar charges. These are not anniversaries which merit public attention, but they do, for better or worse (or rather, for better *and* worse), count in my personal history, for I have now written books on both cases.

It has never been fully established how many people Nilsen killed. Forensic evidence revealed at least 11 victims (three whose remains were still in his flat, and eight whose fragmented skeletons were disinterred from the garden of a house he had occupied earlier), and there may have been as many as 15; some are still unidentified, and are likely to remain so. Dahmer admitted to 17 murders and was eventually charged with 16 of them; all his victims have been identified.

The threads which link these two series of crimes, 5,000 miles apart, are powerful enough to make one stop and wonder. Nilsen and Dahmer stalked men up to the age of 30, men with little or no décor to their lives, men whose families might long since have lost touch with them, and whose disappearance might pass unnoticed. They persuaded these forlorn figures to accompany them home, drugged them (Nilsen with alcohol, Dahmer with alcohol and sleeping pills), strangled them (Nilsen with a tie or string, Dahmer manually or with a strap), and enjoyed the company of their corpses. They both indulged in long, obsessive sessions spent photographing the bodies, creating their own pornography, and both dismembered these people they had briefly known, boiling the heads and sometimes smashing the rest to splinters.

They each had mundane jobs which they were able to pursue even as they lived in the midst of human debris (Nilsen at a JobCentre, Dahmer in a chocolate factory), and each had pets (Nilsen a mongrel dog, Dahmer a tank of exotic fish). In neither case did they appear alarming or dangerous – on the contrary, they were rather to be pitied for their manifest emotional isolation. What the world did not know, until it was too late, was that they had both compensated for a deprivation of affective contact by structuring a secret, alternative life into which strayed people who, to them, were reduced to being no more than props in their private fantasies.

These are unpleasant stories, often so painful to contemplate that the writer who ventures professionally into this perverted world must protect himself from a poisoning of the imagination. The question is bound to arise, then, why do it at all? It is a question often put to me, because I had had no training in psychiatry or criminology, no experience of trials or prisons, no exposure to nastily aberrant behaviour. Before Nilsen, my previous books had been critical studies of French literature and historical or literary biographies, as well as a jolly history of dukedoms – hardly obvious preparation for an excursion into human depravity.

On the other hand, I had always been interested in extreme exemplars of human weakness: Marie Corelli the extreme in literary vanity, Laura Corrigan, the extreme in snobbery, and so on. The little I could glean from initial newspaper reports following Nilsen's arrest suggested all kinds of extremes – in revenge, frustration, loneliness and iniquity – and I suspected that a study of his crimes might elucidate some parts of the tormented baggage we all carry.

Not realising that the Home Office frowned upon people such as myself making contact with prisoners on remand, I wrote to Nilsen at Brixton prison indicating interest "in the case in which you find yourself involved" (at least I understood the presumption of innocence), to which he replied, warning me that if I did pursue the matter, I was likely to find it acutely distressing.

The choice of word intrigued me, for such people are not supposed to know what distress is. It indicated a man who had some appreciation of the immutable Manichaean opposites – light and darkness, good and evil, right and wrong – and chose, whether deliberately or compulsively one could not yet tell the immoral way.

I visited him for the eight months preceding his trial, during which he wrote 50 volumes of notes in his cell, which contributed to the archive I would use in assembling material for my book. I was also present at the trial (and came narrowly close to being recruited to sit with the defendant in the dock, when Nilsen dismissed his lawyer and threatened to defend himself). I have continued to visit him since his conviction. Is this perhaps a little too close? Does one not risk becoming a spokesman, a mouthpiece for wickedness? I think not. It is only by allowing one's self to see the world through the murderer's eyes that one can hope to discover anything helpful about his conduct. Moral certitude and obtuseness are useless encumbrances. To stand at a distance, point the finger, and hurl angry, offended words is perfectly natural, but serves only the need for retribution and assuagement of hurt. One may be inquisitive without becoming an ally, explanatory without making excuses.

Still, murder was not a subject to which I wished to return. Once was enough. Apart from occasionally reviewing books on other cases. I wrote about India, John Aspinall, the Sixties, and E.F. Benson, all unrelated to repetitive addictive homicide. Then came Dahmer, and the identity of method, manner and motive was too obvious to deny.

Oddly enough, the two men are entirely unalike in personality. Nilsen is articulate, intelligent, witty, garrulous, single-minded and stubborn. Dahmer is quiet, polite, monosyllabic, diffident, obliging, intensely private. But this bold disparity is not as important as it may appear. What they have in common is their disorder (and even the most reactionary lover of punishment would not claim these men are perfectly "in order"). They suffer from an emotional perversion, or twisting from the norm, which renders a dead body more beautiful to them than a live one. They are necrophiles.

Such people seem so far removed from ordinary experience that it would seem, on the face of it, that their cases might only be of interest to tabulators and statisticians. Yet there are tiny echoes of normality even in the necrophile, little patches wherein we may recognise ourselves. Are there no men who will admit they have occasionally asked their wives to keep still and simulate unconsciousness during love-making? Are there none who can remember visiting Parisian brothels where whores are trained to behave like corpses, so far as to lying in a coffin? Would not we all, sometimes, prefer an unresisting partner to one who suddenly decides to stop, or points out how ridiculous is the procedure?

I have tried to show how Dahmer's behaviour, from infancy through adolescence, presaged the catastrophe that was to come, to identify the clues which pointed to a necrophilious character – all, of course, with retrospective clarity. Such clues are rarely recognised as such at the time.

When the 12-year-old Dahmer began bringing home the carcasses of animals that had been killed on country roads and asked his father how he might bleach the bones, Lionel Dahmer, a Ph.D. and industrial chemist, was relieved that his son, usually so apathetic and withdrawn, should show an interest in *something*, and probably thought he was destined to be a biologist. He could not be expected to spot signs of incipient necrophilia when they might easily have been innocent, even beneficial. The father did not know that when his son held a living creature, he was feeling how the machine worked inside and where the skeleton fitted, not how cuddly it was. The young Dahmer knew all about the mechanics of an object, and nothing of the love that gave it life. He never would.

It is common enough to assume the best and banish the worst. The father would naturally want to think his son was showing signs of healthy curiosity. Years later, neighbours would want to believe they had not smelt rotting flesh but had detected merely the contents of a faulty freezer. It is the complicity of good manners or decent expectations which the murderer turns to his advantage; in Dahmer's case, even so far as to convince the police to deliver one of his victims to him.

Writing about such people teaches one never to be too certain or cocky about one's moral perspectives. It teaches one also to lend greater weight to the wisdom of mythology and church doctrine which our brutally secular age has neglected. I have never been a religious man, but I have to concede that religious language comes closer to insight than legal, medical or psychiatric jargon. When psychiatrists point to a "personality disorder", they are reluctant to identify the agent of the disorder, when doctors talk of a "chemical imbalance", they avoid saying what caused the imbalance. Ask a priest. He will call it diabolic possession; he will say the devil entered into the murderer's soul and engaged in a fight with the forces of good.

Such a version perfectly matches the accounts given by people who were with Nilsen or Dahmer and lived, people who saw the shadow of hell pass through them. One said that, before the murderous attack, Nilsen had been like a "saint", so caring and encouraging. Tracy Edwards, who escaped from Dahmer and brought about his arrest, said he had been rocking and chanting when in his trance, that his whole body changed.

I am not proposing the devil as a corporeal entity, or even a convincing philosophical premise. I am only saying that it is as good a word as any to describe what is going on. One should be ready to get rid of one's certainties and discover the humility of the perplexed.

If only one of the psychiatrists who appeared in court had had the courage to answer a question with the admission, "I don't know", he would have been secretly embraced by the jurors, struggling with their own ignorance. It is not fanciful to suggest that Dahmer himself might have been relieved, too, as he cannot *know* what brought him to this disastrous end. There is nothing unforgivable about uncertainty in the face of human complexity.

Despite an impression due to popular prejudice, you are not inclined to forget the victims either, those living as well as dead: Carl Stottor, spared by Nilsen, and permanently scarred because he cannot make up his mind whether Nilsen was his murderer or his saviour, being both. Nilsen's mother, still sunk in disbelief and pondering every day. Theresa Smith, after hearing evidence in the courtroom in Milwaukee that her brother Eddie's head had been placed in the oven and exploded, sitting next to me and quietly showing me snapshots of Eddie smiling, Eddie lounging, Eddie leaning against the door, Eddie being alive. The shattering bewilderment of Lionel Dahmer. I could never be indifferent to the suffering caused by the madmen I have written about.

Which raises the question addressed in both courtrooms. How do you measure madness? Common sense will not do, because it is circular (he must be mad to have done